CONSTITUTIONAL
AMENDMENTS
BEYOND THE BILL OF RIGHTS

Amendment XXII
Establishing Term Limits
for U.S. President

Other Books of Related Interest

Opposing Viewpoints Series

American Values

Civil Liberties

Political Campaigns

The U.S. Supreme Court

Current Controversies Series

Federal Elections

The U.S. Economy

CONSTITUTIONAL
AMENDMENTS
BEYOND THE BILL OF RIGHTS

Amendment XXII
Establishing Term Limits
for U.S. President

Tracey Biscontini, Book Editor

GREENHAVEN PRESS
A part of Gale, Cengage Learning

GALE
CENGAGE Learning™

Detroit • New York • San Francisco • New Haven, Conn • Waterville, Maine • London

Christine Nasso, *Publisher*
Elizabeth Des Chenes, *Managing Editor*

© 2010 Greenhaven Press, a part of Gale, Cengage Learning.

Gale and Greenhaven Press are registered trademarks used herein under license.

For more information, contact:
Greenhaven Press
27500 Drake Rd.
Farmington Hills, MI 48331-3535
Or you can visit our Internet site at gale.cengage.com

For product information and technology assistance, contact us at

Gale Customer Support, 1-800-877-4253
For permission to use material from this text or product, submit all requests online at www.cengage.com/permissions

Further permissions questions can be emailed to permissionrequest@cengage.com

Articles in Greenhaven Press anthologies are often edited for length to meet page require- ments. In addition, original titles of these works are changed to clearly present the main thesis and to explicitly indicate the author's opinion. Every effort is made to ensure that Greenhaven Press accurately reflects the original intent of the authors. Every effort has been made to trace the owners of copyrighted material.

Cover photograph © Historical/Corbis.

LIBRARY OF CONGRESS CATALOGING-IN-PUBLICATION DATA

Amendment XXII : establishing term limits for U.S. president / Tracey Biscontini, book editor.
    p. cm. -- (Constitutional amendments: beyond the Bill of Rights)
    Includes bibliographical references and index.
    ISBN 978-0-7377-4452-1 (hardcover) -- ISBN 978-0-7377-5064-5 (pbk.)
    1. Presidents--Term of office--United States. 2. United States. Congress--Term of office. 3. United States. Constitution. 22nd Amendment--History. 4. Constitu- tional amendments--United States. I. Biscontini, Tracey Vasil. II. Title: Amend- ment 22. III. Title: Amendment twenty-two.
    KF5081.A86 2010
    342.73'062--dc22
                                                                    2009040558

Printed in the United States of America
1 2 3 4 5 6 7 14 13 12 11 10

Contents

Chapter 1: Historical Views on Amendment XXII

Chapter 2: Issues Related to Term Limits

   With the New York City Council's overturning of the
   two-term law for New York City's mayoral seat, Mayor
   Michael Bloomberg hopes to seek and win a third term
   in office, enabling his experience as mayor of the city for
   the past seven years and his financial background to help
   New York overcome financial hardship during challenging times.

Appendix

Establishing Term Limits for U.S. President

> *"Today's Constitution is a realistic document of freedom only because of several corrective amendments. Those amendments speak to a sense of decency and fairness."*
>
> *Thurgood Marshall*

While the U.S. Constitution forms the backbone of American democracy, the amendments make the Constitution a living, ever-evolving document. Interpretation and analysis of the Constitution inform lively debate in every branch of government, as well as among students, scholars, and all other citizens, and views on various articles of the Constitution have changed over the generations. Formally altering the Constitution, however, can happen only through the amendment process. The Greenhaven Press series The Bill of Rights examines the first ten amendments to the Constitution. Constitutional Amendments: Beyond the Bill of Rights continues the exploration, addressing key amendments ratified since 1791.

The process of amending the Constitution is painstaking. While other options are available, the method used for nearly every amendment begins with a congressional bill that must pass both the Senate and the House of Representatives by a two-thirds majority. Then the amendment must be ratified by three-quarters of the states. Many amendments have been proposed since the Bill of Rights was adopted in 1791, but only seventeen have been ratified.

It may be difficult to imagine a United States where women and African Americans are prohibited from voting, where the federal government allows one human being to enslave another, or where some citizens are denied equal protection under the law. While many of our most fundamental liberties are protected by the Bill of Rights, the amendments that followed have significantly broadened and enhanced the rights of American citizens. Such rights may be taken for granted today, but when the amendments were ratified, many were considered groundbreaking and proved to be explosively controversial.

Each volume in Constitutional Amendments provides an in-depth exploration of an amendment and its impact through primary and secondary sources, both historical and contemporary. Primary sources include landmark Supreme Court rulings, speeches by prominent experts, and newspaper editorials. Secondary sources include historical analyses, law journal articles, book excerpts, and magazine articles. Each volume first presents the historical background of the amendment, creating a colorful picture of the circumstances surrounding the amendment's passage: the campaigns to sway public opinion, the congressional debates, and the struggle for ratification. Next, each volume examines the ways the court system has been used to test the validity of the amendment and addresses the ramifications of the amendment's passage. The final chapter of each volume presents viewpoints that explore current controversies and debates relating to ways in which the amendment affects our everyday lives.

Numerous features are included in each Constitutional Amendments volume:

- An originally written introduction presents a concise yet thorough overview of the amendment.

- A time line provides historical context by describing key events, organizations, and people relating to the ratification of the amendment, subsequent court cases, and the impact of the amendment.

- An annotated table of contents offers an at-a-glance summary of each primary and secondary source essay included in the volume.

- The complete text of the amendment, followed by a "plain English" explanation, brings the amendment into clear focus for students and other readers.

- Graphs, charts, tables, and maps enhance the text.

- A list of all twenty-seven Constitutional Amendments offers quick reference.

- An annotated list of court cases relevant to the amendment broadens the reader's understanding of the judiciary's role in interpreting the Constitution.

- A bibliography of books, periodicals, and Web sites aids readers in further research.

- A detailed subject index allows readers to quickly find the information they need.

With the aid of this series, students and other researchers will become better informed of their rights and responsibilities as American citizens. Constitutional Amendments: Beyond the Bill of Rights examines the roots of American democracy, bringing to life the ways the Constitution has evolved and how it has impacted this nation's history.

Amendment Text and Explanation

The Twenty-second Amendment to the U.S. Constitution

Section 1. No person shall be elected to the office of the President more than twice, and no person who has held the office of President, or acted as President, for more than two years of a term to which some other person was elected President shall be elected to the office of the President more than once. But this Article shall not apply to any person holding the office of President when this Article was proposed by the Congress, and shall not prevent any person who may be holding the office of President, or acting as President, during the term within which this Article becomes operative from holding the office of President or acting as President during the remainder of such term.

Explanation

Amendment XXII of the U.S. Constitution limits the tenure of the President of the United States to two four-year terms. Ratified by two-thirds of the states in 1951, the amendment says that no individual can be elected to the office of the president more than two times or more than once if he has served more than two years of a previous president's term. The text goes on to say that the amendment does not prevent anyone holding the office of U.S. president when the amendment was proposed or during the time it takes to be implemented from finishing out his term. The objective of the Twenty-second Amendment is to limit presidential tenure to ensure that the executive office does not become a monarchy or dictatorship controlled by one individual.

The process to adopt an amendment that limited presidential tenure came about after President Franklin Delano Roosevelt was elected to a fourth four-year term in 1944. Until Roosevelt, most presidents followed a two-term tradition set by President George Washington in 1796. Washington was elected to two terms in the presidency and retired after completion of his second term, without seeking reelection to a third. Subsequent presidents followed the precedent set by Washington, but a law did not exist to limit the tenure of the president until Amendment XXII was ratified.

Introduction

The idea of term limits for government positions has been in existence since ancient Greece, where average citizens were drawn by lottery to serve for a designated amount of time before they were replaced by other citizens. This process ensured a rotation of office to maintain a democratic society. Because many of the American founding fathers studied ancient democracy in an attempt to establish a democratic society in the New World, the concept of a rotation in office carried over to the early days of the United States.

As early as the first Constitutional Convention in Philadelphia in 1787, the founding fathers extensively discussed the concept of term limits for the presidency. Spearheading the idea of a rotation of office was Thomas Jefferson, who believed that without legislation to govern the term of the presidency, the office would turn into "a position for life." America's founding fathers did not want a monarchy or dictatorship to exist in their new country, but they could not decide on a tenure that would be sufficient for the office of the president. George Washington, for example, did not completely agree with his friend Thomas Jefferson's opinions on the necessity of rotation in the executive department. Washington said he could see no propriety "in precluding ourselves from the services of any man who, in some great emergency, shall be decreed universally most capable of serving the public."

Just as these two men could not agree on term limits, neither could the rest of the delegation. Much discussion revolved around what would be an appropriate amount of time to accomplish all of the things on a president's agenda, but not so much time that an unsatisfactory individual could do harm to the country. Some thought that a single term of six or seven years would be beneficial, while others thought that four years with the option of being reelected would give the

American people more choice. The debate ended on September 15, 1787, when the convention agreed upon a four-year term with election by an electoral college and no restriction on reeligibility. A staunch opponent of term limits was Alexander Hamilton, who in *Federalist* No. 72 argued that limiting the term of the chief executive would diminish accountability, diminish the president's incentive to enact progressive programs, and deny the nation the experience and expertise of a seasoned veteran in the executive office.

George Washington, elected as the first president of the United States in 1789, served for four years and was then reelected to serve four more. After his second term in office ended, Washington decided to retire to Mount Vernon for some much-needed rest. In his farewell address he stated, "To the relation which binds a dutiful citizen to his country, and that in withdrawing the tender of service, which silence in my situation might imply, I am influenced by no diminution of zeal for your future interest; no deficiency of grateful respect for your past kindness, but am supported by a full conviction that the step is comparable with both." Although he did not intend to limit the tenure of future presidents, Washington set a two-term precedent for the executive office.

In the years that followed, subsequent presidents followed suit and did not seek a third term in office. Many believed that the two-term tradition started by Washington should be upheld, and none challenged it until the election of 1940. That year, President Franklin Delano Roosevelt won a third term as president. The country had just dug itself out of the Great Depression, and Roosevelt felt that breaking the two-term tradition was necessary to keep the country's economy stable and to keep the United States out of the war that had begun in Europe. As Roosevelt stated to Democrats at a 1937 dinner, "My great ambition on January 20, 1941, is to turn over my desk and chair in the White House to my successor whoever he may be, with the assurance that I am at the same time turning over to him as President, a Nation intact, a Nation at peace, a Nation prosperous." However, as World War II progressed, Roosevelt felt that he still had work to accomplish for the country and ran for a third term. He won the election of 1940 with 55 percent of the vote and thirty-eight of forty-eight states, which seemed to indicate that the American people did not mind the breaking of the two-term tradition.

In 1944, with the United States engaged in a world war, Roosevelt ran for a fourth term and won 53 percent of the vote and thirty-six states. He died in office several months later, but the tradition of two terms in the executive office had been broken, and not without repercussions.

Not long after Roosevelt's death and the end of World War II, the question of presidential term limits resurfaced—more than one hundred years after its debate at the Constitutional Convention. After two decades of Democratic rule in the White House, the Republican Party, which held majorities in the House of Representatives and the Senate, felt positive that it was time to add a term limit amendment to the Constitution.

On January 3, 1947, Congressmen Earl Michener and Joseph Martin introduced House Joint Resolution 27 (H.J. Res. 27), an amendment limiting the presidential term of office. H.J. Res. 27 stated that "no person shall be chosen or serve as President of the United States for any term, or be eligible to hold the office of President during any term, if such person shall have heretofore served as President during the whole or any part of each of any two separate terms." The House approved the resolution on February 6, 1947, by a vote of 285 to 121. Many Democrats, who believed that the resolution was "anti-Roosevelt," protested the resolution, claiming that it was meant to discredit the New Deal president's legacy and progressive works. Most Democrats in the House and Senate opposed the resolution, but with momentum from the Republicans, the measure was fast on its way to becoming part of the Constitution.

The Senate received H.J. Res. 27 as approved by the House on February 7, 1947, and referred the measure to the Senate Judiciary Committee for review. After much deliberation and debate, and with moderate rewording of the measure, the Senate approved the resolution in a 59-to-23 vote, on March 12, 1947. The Senate's reworded version of the resolution read, "No person shall be elected to the office of the President more than twice, and no person who has held the office of the President, or acted as President, for more than two years of a term to which some other person was elected President, shall be elected to the office of the President more than once." The Senate returned the measure to the House, and after several days of debate, the House adopted the Senate's version of the amendment and sent it to the states for ratification.

From March 24, 1947, to the end of the year, eighteen state legislatures ratified the amendment. Between 1948 and 1950, only six states joined in ratification. It was not until 1951 that the required two-thirds of the states approved the proposed amendment. On May 4, 1951, Alabama ratified the amendment, thus making H.J. Res. 27 the Twenty-second Amendment to the United States Constitution.

The first president affected by Amendment XXII was Dwight Eisenhower. Eisenhower was elected in 1952 and re-elected in 1956. Eisenhower did not favor the amendment, stating that America should "be able to choose for its president anybody that it wants regardless of the number of terms he has served." Former president Harry S. Truman reiterated Eisenhower's sentiments on Amendment XXII when he appeared before the Senate Judiciary Committee's Subcommittee on Constitutional Amendments in 1959, urging a repeal of the amendment. Truman stated that Amendment XXII put the president "in the hardest job in the world . . . with one hand tied behind his back." Many opponents of the amendment, such as Truman and Eisenhower, argued that the two-term president's inability to run for a third term diminishes his power and creates a "lame duck" presidency in the second term. The president's influence over Congress wanes and the authority of the executive branch weakens, they maintained, causing the president to lose the ability to set his own agenda.

Another president who voiced concern about Amendment XXII was Ronald Reagan, who vowed to fight for repeal of the amendment after he left office. Reagan was elected president in 1980 and was reelected in a landslide election in 1984. Halfway through his second term in office, Reagan questioned Amendment XXII, stating, "We ought to take a serious look and see if we haven't interfered with the democratic rights of the people." Although Reagan alluded to running for a third term, his age—78 years at the end of his second term—and Amendment XXII prevented him from doing so.

In recent years, particularly with the popularity of President Bill Clinton in the late 1990s, there has been debate about the interaction between the Twenty-second Amendment and the Twelfth Amendment, which states that "no person constitutionally ineligible to the office of President shall be eligible to that of Vice-President of the United States." In the 2000 election speculation arose that Democratic presidential candidate Al Gore would choose popular former president Bill Clinton as his vice presidential running mate. Many argued that Amendment XXII would prevent this from happening, since a president who has served two full terms is ineligible to be president again; however, this condition exists only if he is *elected* president, not if he *serves* as president. Many contend that for a former president to serve as a vice president—and subsequently as president if need be—is not a violation of Amendment XXII, because the former president would not be *elected* to the presidency. Although a case such as this would not violate the Twenty-second Amendment legally, it would go against the spirit of the amendment and the two-term tradition started by George Washington.

Since its ratification in 1951, numerous calls have been made to repeal Amendment XXII. In 1957 alone, members of the House of Representatives introduced five resolutions to repeal the amendment. Between 1971 and 1973, a growing movement called for a single, six-year term of office for the presidency. Former president Lyndon B. Johnson endorsed this idea after his term of office ended in 1969. Although the proposal had a great deal of support, it failed to pass. In the years since, both Democrats and Republicans have made several unsuccessful attempts to repeal the Twenty-second Amendment. Despite repeated challenges, Amendment XXII remains in place today, limiting presidents to two four-year terms. The amendment sets this limitation in tenure to ensure a rotation in the executive office that many of the founding fathers argued was necessary to retain a free and democratic society.

Chronology

1787

The question of whether the nation's chief executive should be permitted to succeed himself in office is considered at length during the Constitutional Convention in Philadelphia. In September the convention agrees to a four-year term with election by an electoral college and no restriction on reeligibility.

1788

On April 28 George Washington writes a letter to the Marquis de Lafayette in which he states that he does not completely agree with the necessity of rotation in the executive department.

On May 2 Thomas Jefferson writes to Washington that he feels great concern over the possible reeligibility of the president under the Constitution. "This I fear, will make that an office for life, first, and then hereditary." Jefferson advocated a constitutional amendment that would fix the presidential term at seven years and declare the president ineligible for reelection.

1789

George Washington is unanimously elected the first president of the United States by the electoral college.

1792

Washington is elected for a second term as president.

1796

In his "Farewell Address" published on September 17, Washington expresses his desire to retire and not be a candidate for another term. With this refusal to run for a third term, a presidential two-term tradition is founded and continues until 1940.

1800

The presidential election is resolved by Congress since Thomas Jefferson and Aaron Burr receive an equal number of electoral votes. The House chooses Jefferson as president, and Burr becomes vice president.

1803

Resolutions are introduced in Congress recommending constitutional amendments prohibiting a third presidential term. Among these is a resolution debated in the Senate "that no person who has been twice successively elected President of the United States shall be eligible as President until four years shall have elapsed [after which he may] be eligible to the office of President for four years and no longer." The resolution is rejected in the Senate by a vote of 4 to 25.

1804

The Twelfth Amendment is ratified and adopted. This amendment provides the procedure by which the president and vice president are elected. There is no attempt in this amendment to limit the terms served by a president.

1824

The Senate passes a joint resolution providing that no man should be chosen president for more than two terms. No action is taken on this resolution in the House.

The presidential election is again resolved by Congress, and John Quincy Adams is chosen president by the House. He serves only one term.

1826

The contested election of 1824 produces many joint resolutions recommending amendments to the Constitution on the method of presidential election and the length of the presidential term. One of these resolutions, advocating a limit of two terms for the president, is passed in the Senate by a vote of 32 to 7; however, nothing is done with the resolution in the House.

1828

Andrew Jackson is elected president.

1829

In his first annual message to Congress, Jackson recommends that the electoral college be abolished, that the president be elected by direct vote, and that the president be limited to a single term of either four or six years.

1840

William Henry Harrison is elected president. In his inaugural speech in March 1841, he affirms his recommendation for a single presidential term. He dies a month later, and John Tyler becomes the first vice president to assume the presidency.

1865

President Abraham Lincoln is assassinated and is succeeded by vice president Andrew Johnson, who suggests to Congress a single term for the president.

1875

On December 15 the House passes a resolution, introduced by Democrat William M. Springer of Illinois. The resolution indicates that retirement from office after two terms is a "time-honored custom" and that any departure from this tradition is "unwise, unpatriotic, and fraught with peril to our free institutions."

1876

Rutherford B. Hayes is elected president, and in his first inaugural address in 1877 he recommends an amendment to the Constitution limiting the president to a single term of six years.

1877

A resolution is introduced based on President Hayes's recommendation of a single six-year term. No action is taken.

1880

In the Republican National Convention, Ulysses S. Grant is seriously considered for a third term, with many people convinced that the lapse of four years between Grant's last service as president made him reeligible for office. Grant leads all other candidates on thirty-five ballots, but ultimately James Garfield is nominated and elected. President Garfield is assassinated in 1881, and vice president Chester A. Arthur becomes president.

1884

Grover Cleveland is elected president.

1888

Cleveland is renominated as the Democratic candidate but is defeated by the Republican candidate, Benjamin Harrison.

1892

Cleveland is reelected to a second term.

1896

The Democratic platform declares "the unwritten law of this Republic, established by custom and usage of 100 years, and sanctioned by the example of the greatest and wisest of those who founded and maintained our Government, that no man should be eligible for a third term of the Presidential office."

William McKinley is elected in 1896 and reelected in 1900. Shortly after his second inauguration in 1901, President McKinley is the subject of third-term speculation, but that soon diminishes after he issues a public statement saying he would not seek a third term.

1901

President McKinley is assassinated and is succeeded by vice president Theodore Roosevelt.

1904

The incumbent Theodore Roosevelt is elected president. Shortly after his victory, Roosevelt announces that he regards his service after McKinley's assassination as his first term and that he would not seek reelection for a third term.

1913

On February 1, before the first inauguration of President Woodrow Wilson, the Senate passes a joint resolution known as the Works' resolution (after Sen. John D. Works), providing for a constitutional amendment limiting the president to a single six-year term. No action is taken on the resolution in the House.

President Wilson does not approve of the resolution and states "that he would abide by the judgment of his party and the people as to whether he would be a candidate for reelection in 1916."

1932

Franklin D. Roosevelt is elected the thirty-second president of the United States.

1936

Roosevelt is voted into the office of president for a second term.

1939–1943

Five separate Senate resolutions are introduced to limit presidential tenure and discourage Roosevelt from running for president again. No action is taken on any of these.

1940

Roosevelt is elected to a third term as president. He is the only president to serve more than two terms.

1944

Franklin D. Roosevelt is elected to a fourth term as president. He dies several months later, in April 1945. Vice president Harry S. Truman becomes president.

1947

On January 3 House Joint Resolution 27 (later to become Amendment XXII) is introduced in the House. This resolution states, "Any person who has served as President of the United States during all or portions of any two terms, shall thereafter be ineligible to hold the office of President."

On February 6 the joint resolution is passed in the House by a vote of 285 to 121.

On February 7 the proposal is referred to the Senate Committee on the Judiciary.

On March 7 another joint resolution is offered in the Senate. It fixes the maximum tenure of all elected federal officers to six years, with eligibility for reelection. It is defeated by a margin of 82 to 1.

On March 12 the House Joint Resolution 27 is passed in the Senate by a vote of 59 to 23. The resolution is changed, however, with approval from the House, to read, "no person shall be elected to the office of the President more than twice, and no person who has held the office of President, or acted as President, for more than two years of a term to which some other person was elected President shall be elected to the office of the President more than once."

On March 24 the House Committee on House Administration files House Joint Resolution 27 with the secretary of state for transmittal to state legislatures.

By the end of May, eighteen states have ratified the amendment. These states are Maine, Michigan, Iowa, Kansas, New Hampshire, Oregon, Illinois, Delaware, Vermont, California, New Jersey, Wisconsin, Ohio, Colorado, Pennsylvania, Nebraska, Missouri, and Connecticut.

1948

Only three states, Virginia, Mississippi, and New York, ratify the amendment in this year.

1949

North Dakota and South Dakota ratify the amendment.

1950

Louisiana ratifies the amendment in May.

1951

Early in the year, thirteen states—Montana, Indiana, Idaho, New Mexico, Wyoming, Arkansas, Georgia, Tennessee, Texas, Nevada, Utah, Minnesota, and North Carolina—ratify the amendment. By May, South Carolina, Maryland, Florida, and Alabama vote for ratification of House Joint Resolution 27, making it the Twenty-second Amendment to the U.S. Constitution.

1952

Dwight D. Eisenhower is elected president. He is the first president subject to the two-term limitation of Amendment XXII.

1956

Two resolutions are introduced in the House to repeal the Twenty-second Amendment.

1957

Five resolutions are introduced in the House to repeal the Twenty-second Amendment.

1959

The House and Senate hold hearings on the Twenty-second Amendment and consider its repeal.

1971

Senators George D. Aiken (R-Vermont) and Mike Mansfield (D-Montana) introduce a constitutional amendment to establish a single six-year term for the presidency. It is not passed.

1986

Rep. Guy Vander Jagt (R-Michigan) introduces legislation to repeal the Twenty-second Amendment, so as to allow President Ronald Reagan to run for a third term.

1995

A joint resolution is introduced to the Committee on the Judiciary by Senator Mitch McConnell (R-Kentucky) to repeal the Twenty-second Amendment.

2005

Rep. Steny Hoyer (D-Maryland) introduces a resolution to repeal Amendment XXII; it receives little backing.

CONSTITUTIONAL
AMENDMENTS
BEYOND THE BILL OF RIGHTS

CHAPTER 1

Historical Views on Amendment XXII

Interest in Term Limits Has Existed Since Revolutionary Times

Joseph E. Kallenbach

In the following viewpoint, Joseph E. Kallenbach explains that a long continuance in office has been a matter of contention in American political thinking since the Revolution in the late eighteenth century. Kallenbach asserts that even though the states recognized the importance of limiting executive power—seven of the original thirteen state constitutions limited the number of times an individual could serve as the state's chief executive— the framers of the U.S. Constitution had a difficult time coming to an agreement on presidential tenure. The state legislatures, by limiting the terms of office of the chief executive, conveyed a widely held belief that a rotation in office was necessary to preserve a democratic and free society. According to Kallenbach, many of the framers of the Constitution felt that a single term of six or eight years would be feasible if Congress elected the president; others believed that a popular vote by the people could impose a shorter term with reeligibility for the executive office. Kallenbach (1903–1991) was a political science professor at the University of Michigan who wrote several books on American government.

On March 1, 1951, the Administrator of General Services certified that the proposed presidential tenure amendment submitted to the states by Congress in 1947 had been ratified by thirty-six states, thus making it a part of the United States Constitution. Adoption of this proposal, which becomes the Twenty-second Amendment to the United States Constitu-

Joseph E. Kallenbach, "Constitutional Limitations on Reeligibility of National and State Chief Executives," *The American Political Science Review*, vol. 46, no. 2, June 1952, pp. 438–54.

tion, disposes of an issue that has agitated American politics periodically since the establishment of the Presidency. Hereafter no person will be eligible for a third term as President if he has served two full elective terms or one full elective term plus more than one-half of another term through succession to the office. President [Harry S.] Truman, who would otherwise be rendered ineligible for reelection following completion of his current term, is exempted from the ban by a qualifying clause which excludes from coverage "any person holding the office of President when this Article was proposed by the Congress."

Hostility to long continuance in office, particularly for executive officers, has been a prominent feature of American political thinking since Revolutionary times. Seven of the original state constitutions, all of which were formulated prior to adoption of the federal Constitution, carried clauses limiting reeligibility of the state chief executive. These provisions reflected a widely-held belief that a rotation in executive office was essential to the preservation of liberty. A sectional preference for the principle of limitation was noticeable; for it was found only in the constitutions of the group of states lying from Pennsylvania to the southward. The method by which the governor was chosen was evidently a factor in the situation. Legislative selection was the mode of choice in all of the seven states where limitations on reelection were imposed; while New Jersey was the only state employing this mode of selection without imposing also a tenure restriction. In the four New England states and New York, where the governor was chosen by popular election, there were no provisions barring reelection. Prevention of intrigue and bargaining with the legislature by a governor intent upon securing his own continuance in office seems to have been a major objective of these early state constitutional restrictions on reeligibility. A survey of the record demonstrates that continuation of chief executives in office for term after term was by no means

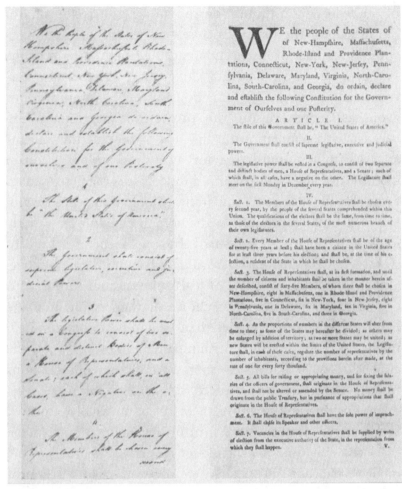

Two drafts of the Constitution of the United States of America, 1787. Photo by Kean Collection/Getty Images.

viewed everywhere as dangerous in Revolutionary times. In those states where tenure limitations were lacking, repeated reelections of governors were common during the Revolutionary period and immediately after.

The Question of Reeligibility

These differences in attitudes and practices among the original states help to explain the vacillations of the framers of the federal Constitution on the question of reeligibility of the President. The issue was closely associated in their minds with the manner of his election and the length of term. If the President was to be chosen by Congress, it was generally conceded that a reeligibility limitation was necessary in order to avoid, as George Mason [one of the founding fathers] expressed it, "a temptation on the side of the Executive to intrigue with the Legislature for a re-appointment." Consequently the advocates of this mode of selection tended to favor also the idea of a comparatively long term, since only in this way could continuity in the administration over a fairly long period of time be assured. Establishment of a term of six, seven, or eight years accordingly became their objective. Opponents of the principle of legislative selection emphasized the point that to place the choice of the President in the hands of an authority other than Congress would eliminate the necessity for a reeligibility limitation and make feasible the establishment of a relatively short term. These considerations were undoubtedly factors of considerable importance in inducing acceptance of the plan of selection finally adopted. While a few members were firm in their conviction that the President should not be eligible for reelection regardless of the mode of selection and others were opposed to a limitation of this nature in any case, the controlling factor in the minds of a decisive majority of the Convention on the point of reeligibility was whether his election was to be achieved through Congress or by some other mode.

The lack of a clause limiting the reeligibility of the President was a point advanced against the Constitution by some of its critics during the ratification struggle. [Alexander] Hamilton felt obliged to devote the major part of one of the *Federalist Papers* to a defense of the Convention's conclusions on this point. Three of the state conventions adopted recommendations that Congress should immediately submit to the states an amendment establishing a limitation on presidential tenure, but the First Congress failed to act in accordance with these recommendations.

The fact that the idea of tenure restriction was associated so closely with the device of legislative election in the thinking of many of the founding fathers suggests that as popular election was substituted for legislative selection in the choosing of state governors, constitutional restrictions on reeligibility would be relaxed or abandoned. A trend in this direction did become manifest in the decade following the adoption of the Constitution. . . .

The principle of rotation in office was a cardinal point in the lexicon of Jeffersonian [after Thomas Jefferson] and Jacksonian [after Andrew Jackson] democratic thought. As elements deriving their political philosophy from these leaders became dominant in American politics, their thinking was reflected in constitutional developments relating to executive tenure and reeligibility at both the national and state levels of government. Jefferson's refusal to seek a third term as President on grounds of principle laid the foundation for the "two-term tradition" with respect to that office. In 1824 and again in 1826 the Senate passed constitutional amendment proposals designed to incorporate this rule in the written Constitution. Although Jackson accepted a second nomination and election to the Presidency, he repeatedly urged the adoption of a constitutional amendment limiting a President to a single term of four or six years. Meanwhile, as the remaining original states which had at first embraced the legislative election device for choosing their governors changed to the system of popular election, they saw fit to retain strict limitations on reeligibility. . . .

Most States Limit Terms

By 1850 approximately two-thirds of the states had constitutional limitations of this character. A sectional preference for the idea, as in Revolutionary times, was still discernible. The states with restrictions included all those, with the exception of Georgia, comprising the block extending from Pennsylvania and New Jersey to the South and West. The six New England states, New York, Michigan, Wisconsin, and Iowa, along with Georgia, were the only ones in which the idea of a rotation in office, enforced by constitutional rule, had failed to win acceptance. In most of the states with restrictive clauses at that time, the prohibition was in the form of a limit of one term of two, three, or four years. It is significant that by 1860 a one-term tradition with regard to the office of President seemed also in process of establishment. Most of the amendment proposals designed to limit presidential tenure introduced in Congress from 1825 to 1860 were directed to this end. No President from the time of Jackson to [Abraham] Lincoln, a period covering seven full presidential terms, was able to win reelection and only one, [Martin] Van Buren, obtained renomination by his party for a second term. In his inaugural address in 1841, President [William Henry] Harrison pledged himself to one term only, and the Whig party's platform of 1844 endorsed the single-term principle. . . .

Near the close of President [Ulysses S.] Grant's second administration suggestions began to be heard from some quarters in his party that he should be renominated for a third term. Opposition to the suggestion at once was quickly voiced by elements within the Republican party as well as by the rival party. On December 15, 1875, the House of Representatives passed by a vote of 234 to 18 a resolution introduced by Representative [William McKendree] Springer, Democrat, declaring that a departure from the two-term tradition would be "unwise, unpatriotic and fraught with peril to our free institutions." Nevertheless, four years later this tradition was subjected to its first serious challenge when in the Republican convention of 1880 a nearly successful effort was made to nominate Grant for what would have been a third, but non-successive, term. . . .

The framers of the Twenty-second Amendment were aware of the problem of the partial term and disposed of it explicitly in the Amendment. The debates over whether Theodore Roosevelt and Calvin Coolidge would have been given "third" terms if they had been elected in 1912 and 1928, respectively, were sufficiently fresh in mind to account for the inclusion of specific language on this point; and the case of President Truman, who was at the time of submission of the Amendment serving out the remainder of F. D. Roosevelt's fourth term, was also directly at hand. Few of the states have had the foresight to deal explicitly with this question in their constitutional provisions. The matter is further complicated by the fact that in a number of states, including New Jersey, Delaware, Kentucky, Georgia, and Oregon, a vacancy in the office of governor occurring during the first part of a four-year term is filled by special election at the next succeeding general election. In all these states except Delaware, the ensuing election is for the unexpired portion of the current term. In Delaware the special election is for a full four-year term. . . .

Why Term Limits Are Favored

The continuing support given to the principle of limited tenure for chief executives, as evidenced in the adoption of the Twenty-second Amendment and in the practices of a considerable number of states, invites inquiry into the factors accounting for its wide acceptance. One of the main considerations which led to its adoption originally has long since vanished with the abandonment of legislative election of chief executives. Modern defenders of the principle of limited tenure, however, are still able to capitalize upon the traditional popular distrust of the executive which had its origins in American experience prior to the Revolution. The modern tendency toward strengthening the legislative and executive powers of chief executives at the national and state levels operates to keep such fears alive. Supporters of tenure limitation therefore continue to stress the arguments that it will tend to give an executive greater freedom from narrow partisan considerations in the conduct of his office; curb his lust for power; free him from the temptation to use his powers, especially the patronage power, to achieve his own renomination and reelection; and in general afford greater security against the threat of "dictatorship." They deny or discount materially the counterarguments that adequate protection is afforded against executive usurpation in a limited term of office, the system of separation of powers, and a written constitution; that the opportunity of securing a vote of confidence from the people by obtaining reelection gives a chief executive a powerful incentive to deport himself with rectitude and administer his office with due consideration to the public interest and desire; and that in time of crisis an enforced rotation in the office of chief executive may be highly undesirable. They ignore the contention that a genuine would-be "dictator" would have ample time to attempt to accomplish his purposes during one term of office, to say nothing of two, and would be as little inclined to respect a written constitutional limitation on his tenure as any other part of the constitutional plan which stood in his way.

While public reaction to the debate on the issue in terms of these arguments accounts in some measure for current practice, considerations of party advantage of the moment, personal politics, the traditional jealousy of legislative bodies toward the executive, and the character of the party system are factors which also help to account for constitutional limitations on the chief executive. The records of the two major parties on the issue since the time of the Civil War have been curiously inconsistent. By and large, up to 1940 the Democratic party had shown more hostility to the idea of unlimited tenure for chief executives than had the Republicans. The two most serious challenges to the anti-third term tradition in connection with the Presidency were made in the Republican conventions of 1880 and 1912; while Democratic members of Congress more consistently supported efforts to prevent its violation than did their Republican colleagues. In most of the states which limit the tenure of governors the Democrats are the majority party. But in the struggle over the Twenty-second Amendment, these party roles were in large measure reversed.

The fact that this proposal came so soon after the two-term tradition had been successfully challenged by a Democratic President gave it the character of a pro-Roosevelt, anti-Roosevelt partisan issue in much the same sense that earlier actions by Congress had reflected anti-Grant, anti-Theodore Roosevelt and anti-Coolidge partisan sentiment. Not a single Republican vote was cast against it in either House of Congress. Those Democrats in Congress who supported it were for the most part identified with the anti-Roosevelt faction of the party. In the first three years of the period in which the Amendment was before the states for ratification, Democratic-controlled legislatures generally showed a reluctance to act favorably upon it, while Republican-dominated legislatures rushed to approve it. Only after political developments in the post-war period had begun to raise increasing doubts in Democratic ranks concerning the soundness of President Roosevelt's judgment as a policy-maker did Democratic-dominated state legislatures display in any numbers a favorable attitude toward the Amendment. During 1950 and 1951 reaction against President Truman's leadership within the Democratic party also played a part in bringing about favorable action in states where this party controlled the legislature, after it came to be realized that adoption of the Amendment might operate in some degree to discourage his seeking reelection in 1952.

The injection of political considerations of a partisan or personal nature into the question of ratification of the presidential tenure proposal accounts for what may be regarded as an inconsistency in the attitude of the states on the basic issue. In general, the legislatures of those states without provisions in their own constitutions limiting reeligibility of their governors displayed greater enthusiasm for the proposal than those of states which have. Of the first 18 states to ratify the Amendment, all of which acted within a few months after its submission, only five had constitutions limiting the tenure of their own chief executives. The legislatures of California and New York were among the earliest to ratify; yet in each of those states a governor who had been one of the standard-bearers of the Republican party in the 1948 presidential election was reelected for a third successive four-year term in 1950. Eventually, all but five of the 27 states which do not have restrictions in their own constitutions on reelection of their governors were numbered among the 36 ratifying states.

Why the Legislature Sought a Constitutional Limit on Tenure

Support of the principle of constitutional limitations on the tenure of chief executives by members of national and state legislative bodies can be explained further by reference to its implications under the system of separation of powers. Separation of powers tends to place the chief executive and the legislative branch in the role of competitors for power and prestige. Legislators are therefore inclined to look with favor upon a device designed to break the grip of any individual who has achieved the position of head of the executive branch. A forced rotation in this office, they reason, will weight the scales on the side of the legislative branch in the struggle between the two. An additional justification for such a rotation from the standpoint of the legislators arises from the fact that the chief executive, for a variety of reasons, has come to be accorded the position of party spokesman and leader. The two major parties are, in the national sense, essentially federalizations of state parties. Even at the state level, they are combinations of local and factional elements which compete among themselves for power within the group. These factional elements of the party, if important enough, are represented in the legislative branch and have their spokesmen there. What is more natural than for the representatives of all these factions except the one temporarily in possession of the executive office to regard with favor a constitutional rule which compels retirement of the party chief at periodic intervals and thus opens the way for advancement to the top for others, particularly when the legislative membership itself usually includes a number who themselves aspire to this higher rung on the political ladder? In the southern states where the contest for the governorship is essentially a struggle between factions within the Democratic party at its primary, a restriction on reeligibility of the chief executive becomes especially significant as a device for disqualifying the incumbent party chieftain in the periodic competition for power. The point is often more euphemistically stated in terms of an argument that rotation in executive office must be enforced to permit the rise of a new leadership. Naturally enough, the legislators who advance this argument see no need to apply this principle to themselves as holders of positions of power and importance in the party hierarchy.

A constitutional restriction on reeligibility is in the final analysis an expression of lack of faith in the electorate's ability to make an intelligent decision on whether to continue in office a chief executive who has had an opportunity to make a record upon which he can be judged. It is a denial of power to the voters to retain in office a chief executive who would otherwise win renomination and reelection, for a fixed term of office provides them with opportunity at periodic intervals to dismiss an unsatisfactory incumbent. Consequently the attitude of the people on the general issue, rather than that of persons of influence in party affairs who may be suspected of reflecting a certain amount of bias arising from their own partisan or personal interests is of particular significance.

The Politics of Amendment XXII

Whether the Twenty-second Amendment is merely a "politician's amendment," introduced into the Constitution by action of national and state legislators who registered only their own partisan and personal views, or was the reflection of a strong, genuine public opinion remains a debatable point. Provision for its reference to popularly chosen state conventions, as was made in the case of submission of the Twenty-first Amendment, was deliberately avoided by its backers in Congress. In view of the fact that the two-term tradition had been repudiated by the voters of the nation by the reelection of President Roosevelt in 1940 and 1944, supporters of the proposal in Congress had good reason to mistrust a ratification method which would have, in effect, permitted a popular referendum, state by state, on the issue. Polls of popular opinion on the issue of maintaining the two-term tradition with reference to the Presidency showed a considerable shifting of attitudes in the nation from 1936 to 1947. Prior to 1937 there was majority support for the two-term principle. Then, in line with the action of the voters in breaking the tradition with the reelection of President Roosevelt in 1940, there was a shift to the contrary view. Republican voters consistently favored the principle by a heavy margin; while Democratic voters opposed it by a somewhat lesser margin. These polls suggest that the Amendment might still have been approved if its ratification had been left to popularly chosen conventions; but the public's attitude on the issue was by no means so clear as to have assured this outcome.

The ultimate effect on the Presidency of the now-formalized rule of compulsory retirement after two terms is difficult to assess. A backward projection gives some indication of its future impact. If the Twenty-second Amendment had been in effect since 1789, it appears that the outcome of two presidential elections in addition to those of 1940 and 1944 would have been affected. If General Grant had not been a strong contender for a third-term nomination in 1880, the "dark horse" Garfield might well have never emerged as the candidate of the Republicans, and the election of that year would probably have placed someone else in the White House. Again in 1912 Theodore Roosevelt would not have been eligible for the Presidency, and the split in the Republican party which resulted from his candidacy and made possible the election of Woodrow Wilson conceivably would not have occurred. Of the 32 persons who have occupied the office of President [as of 1952], ten would have been rendered ineligible for further service. Those who would have been forever disqualified include six of the seven Presidents who are generally recognized as having been our most outstanding and able ones.

Views of Presidents Concerning the Term of Office

Congressional Digest

Several U.S. presidents, either while in office or after their terms were completed, have given their views on the presidential term. The idea of setting term limits for presidents has been the subject of much debate from as far back as George Washington's days in office and even earlier, at the Constitutional Convention in 1787. The following viewpoint from Congressional Digest, *a monthly publication that has presented pro and con views of congressional debates since 1921, reflects the views of several U.S. presidents concerning rotation of the executive office. This article, published in 1938, was pertinent at the time, since much debate surrounded Franklin Delano Roosevelt's consideration to run for a third term, which would break the precedent set by George Washington of limiting the presidency to two four-year terms.*

A number of Presidents, either while they were in office or afterwards, have been called upon to express their views on the subject of the Presidential term. Following are some of the most noteworthy of such statements:

George Washington: First President of the United States, 1789–1797

Letter to [the Marquis de] Lafayette, April 28, 1788: Guarded so effectively as the proposed Constitution is in respect to the promotion of bribery and undue influence in the choice of President, I confess I differ widely myself from Mr. [Thomas] Jefferson and you as to the necessity or expediency of rotation in that department. The matter was freely discussed in the convention and to my full conviction.

Congressional Digest, "Views of Presidents Concerning the Presidential Term," May 1938, vol. 17, no. 5, pp. 140–43.

Though I cannot have time or room to sum up the argument in this letter, there cannot, in my judgment, be the least danger that the President will by any practicable intrigue ever be able to continue himself one moment in office, much less perpetuate himself in it, but in the last stage of corrupt morals and practical depravity, and even then there is as much danger that any species of domination would prevail. Though when a people have become incapable of governing themselves and fit for a master, it is of little consequence from what quarter he comes. Under an extended view of this part of the subject I can see no propriety in precluding ourselves from the services of any man who in some great emergency shall be deemed universally most capable of serving the public.

Farewell Address, September 17, 1796: The period for a new election of a citizen to administer the Executive Government of the United States being not far distant, and the time actually arrived when your thoughts must be employed in designating the person who is to be clothed with that important trust, it appears to me proper, especially as it may conduce to a more distinct expression of the public voice, that I should now apprise you of the resolution I have formed to decline being considered among the number of those out of whom a choice is to be made.

I beg you at the same time to do me the justice to be assured that this resolution has not been taken without a strict regard to all the considerations appertaining to the relation which binds a dutiful citizen to his country, and that in withdrawing the tender of service, which silence in my situation might imply, I am influenced by no diminution of zeal for your future interest; no deficiency of grateful respect for your past kindness, but am supported by a full conviction that the step is compatible with both.

The acceptance of, and continuance hitherto in, the office to which your suffrages have twice called me have been a uni-

George Washington leads the Founding Fathers in the signing of the United States Constitution. ©Bettmann/Corbis.

form sacrifice of inclination to the opinion of duty, and to a deference for what appeared to be your desire. I constantly hoped that it would have been much earlier in my power, consistently with motives with which I am not at liberty to disregard, to return to that retirement from which I had been reluctantly drawn. The strength of my inclination to do this previous to the last election had even led to the preparation of an address to declare it to you, but mature reflection on the then perplexed and critical posture of our affairs with foreign nations, and the unanimous advice of persons entitled to my confidence, impelled me to abandon the idea.

I rejoice that the state of your concerns, external as well as internal, no longer renders the pursuit of inclination incompatible with the sentiment of duty or propriety; and am persuaded, whatever partiality may be retained for my services, that in the present circumstances of our country you will not disapprove my determination to retire.

The impressions with which I first undertook the arduous trust were explained on the proper occasion. . . . Not unconscious in the outset of the inferiority of my qualifications, experience in my own eyes, perhaps still more in the eyes of others, has strengthened the motives to diffidence of myself; and every day the increasing weight of years admonishes me more and more that the shade of retirement is as necessary to me as it will be welcome. Satisfied that, if any circumstances have given peculiar value to my services, they were temporary, I have the consolation to believe that, while choice and prudence invite me to quit the political scene, patriotism does not forbid it.

Thomas Jefferson: Third President of the United States, 1801–1809

Letter to [George] Washington, May 2, 1788: I intended to have written a word to your Excellency on the subject of the new Constitution, but I have already spun out my letter to an immoderate length. I will just observe, therefore, that according to my ideas there is a good deal of good in it. There are two things, however, which I dislike strongly.

First—the want of a Declaration of Rights. I am hoping the opposition of Virginia will remedy this and produce such a declaration.

Second—the perpetual reeligibility of the President. This, I fear, will make an office for life. I was much an enemy of monarchy before I came to Europe. I am ten thousand times more so since I have seen what they are. . . . I shall hope that before there is danger of this change taking place in the office of President the good sense and free spirit of our countrymen will make the change necessary to prevent it. Under this hope I look forward to the general adoption of the new Constitution with anxiety as necessary for us under our present circumstances.

Letter to Vermont Legislature, December 10, 1807: I received in due season the address of the Legislature of Vermont, bearing date of the 5th of November, 1806, in which, with their approbation of the general course of my administration, they were so good as to express their desire that I would consent to be proposed again to the public voice on the expiration of my present term of office. Entertaining as I do for the Legislature of Vermont those sentiments of high respect which would have prompted an immediate answer, I was certain, nevertheless, they would approve a delay which has for its object to avoid a premature agitation of the public mind on a subject so interesting as the election of a Chief Magistrate.

That I should lay down my charge at a proper period is as much a duty as to have borne it faithfully. If some termination to the services of the Chief Magistrate be not fixed by the Constitution, or supplied by practice, his office, nominally for years, will in fact become for life; and history shows how easily that degenerates into an inheritance. Believing that a representative government responsible at short periods of election is that which produces the greatest sum of happiness to mankind, I feel it a duty to do no act which shall essentially impair that principle; and I should unwillingly be the person who, disregarding the sound precedent set by an illustrious predecessor, should furnish the first example of prolongation beyond the second term of office.

Truth also requires me to add that I am sensible of that decline which advancing years bring on, and, feeling their physical, I ought not to doubt their mental effect. Happy if I am the first to perceive and to obey this admonition of nature, and to solicit a retreat from cares too great for the wearied faculties of age.

For the approbation which the Legislature of Vermont has been pleased to express of the principles and measures pursued in the management of their affairs, I am sincerely thankful; and should I be so fortunate as to carry into retirement the equal approbation and good-will of my fellow citizens generally, it will be the comfort of my future days, and will close a service of forty years with the only reward it ever wished.

John Quincy Adams: President of the United States, 1825–1829

Memoirs: They (the principles and arguments against a third term), are sown in the practice which the Virginia Presidents have taken so much pains to engraft on the Constitution, making it a principle that no President can be more than twice elected. This is not a principle of the Constitution, and I am satisfied it ought not to be. Its inevitable consequence is to make every administration a scene of continuous and furious electioneering for the succession to the Presidency.

Andrew Jackson: President of the United States, 1829–1837

Message to Congress, December 1, 1834: I trust that I may be also pardoned for renewing the recommendation I have so often submitted to your attention in regard to the mode of electing the President and Vice-President of the United States. All the reflection I have been able to bestow upon the subject increases my conviction that the best interests of the country will be promoted by the adoption of some plan which will secure in all contingencies that important right of sovereignty to the direct control of the people. Could this be attained, and the terms of those officers be limited to a single period of either four or six years, I think our liberties would possess an additional safeguard.

Rutherford B. Hayes: President of the United States, 1877–1881

Inaugural Address, March 5, 1877: In furtherance of the reform we seek, and in other important respects a change of great importance, I recommend an amendment to the Constitution prescribing a term of six years for the presidential office and forbidding a reelection.

William McKinley: President of the United States, 1897–1901

Public Statement, June 10, 1901: I regret that the suggestion of a third term has been made. I doubt whether I am called upon to give to it notice, but there are new questions of the gravest importance before the administration and the country, and their just consideration should not be prejudiced in the public mind by even the suspicion of the thought of a third term. In view . . . of a long-settled conviction . . . I will not be a candidate for a third term. . . .

Theodore Roosevelt: President of the United States, 1901–1909

Public Statement, November 8, 1904: On the fourth of March next I shall have served three and a half years, and these three and a half years constitute my first term. The wise custom which limits the President to two terms regards the substance, and not the form, and under no circumstances will I be a candidate for or accept another nomination.

Public Statement, February 25, 1912: I will accept the nomination if it is tendered to me, and I will adhere to this decision until the convention has expressed its preference.

William Howard Taft: President of the United States, 1909–1913

"The Presidency," 1916: I am strongly inclined to the view that it would have been a wiser provision, as it was at one time voted in the convention, to make the term of President seven years and render him ineligible thereafter. Such a change would give to the Executive greater courage and independence in the discharge of his duties. The absorbing and diverting interest in the reelection of the incumbent taken by Federal civil servants who regard their own tenure as dependent upon his would disappear and the efficiency of administration in the last year of a term be maintained.

Calvin Coolidge: President of the United States, 1921–1929

Address to Republican National Committee, December 6, 1927: This is naturally the time to be planning the future. The party will soon place in nomination its candidate to succeed me. To give time for mature deliberations I stated to the country on August 2 that I did not choose to run for President in 1928. My statement stands. No one should be led to suppose that I have modified it. My decision will be respected. After I had been eliminated the party began, and should vigorously continue, the serious task of selecting another candidate from the number of distinguished men available.

Woodrow Wilson: President of the United States, 1913–1921

Letter to Representative A. Mitchell Palmer, February 3, 1913: I have not hitherto said anything about this question, because I had not observed that there was any evidence that the public was very much interested in it. I must have been mistaken in this, else the Senate would hardly have acted so promptly upon it.

It is a matter which concerns the character and conduct of the great office upon the duties of which I am about to enter. I feel, therefore, that in the present circumstances I should not be acting consistently with my ideals with regard to the rule of entire frankness and plain speaking that ought to exist between public servants and the public whom they serve if I did not speak out about it without reserve of any kind and without thought of the personal embarrassment.

The question is simply this: Shall our Presidents be free, so far as the law is concerned, to seek a second term of four years, or shall they be limited by Constitutional Amendment to a single term of four years or to a single term extended to six years?

Four years is too long a term for a President who is not the true spokesman of the people, who is imposed upon and does not lead. It is too short for a President who is doing, or attempting a great work of reform, and who has not had time to finish it. To change the term to six years would be to increase the likelihood of its being too long, without any assurance that it would, in happy cases, be long enough. A fixed Constitutional limitation to a single term of office is highly arbitrary and unsatisfactory from every point of view.

The argument for it rests upon temporary conditions which can easily be removed by law. Presidents, it is said, are effective for one-half of their term only because they devote their attention during the last two years of the term to building up the influences, and above all, the organization by which they hope and purpose to secure a second nomination and election.

It is their illicit power, not their legitimate influence with the country, that the advocates of a Constitutional change profess to be afraid of, and I heartily sympathize with them. It is intolerable that any President should be permitted to determine who should succeed him—himself or another—by patronage or coercion, or by any sort of control of the machinery by which delegates to the nominating convention are chosen.

There ought never to be another presidential nominating convention; and there need never be another. Several of the States have successfully solved that difficulty with regard to the choice of their governors, and Federal law can solve it in the same way with regard to the choice of President. The nominations should be made directly by the people.

It must be clear to everybody who has studied our political development at all that the character of the presidency is passing through a transitional stage. We know what the office is now and what use must be made of it; but we do not know what it is going to work out into; and until we do know, we shall not know what Constitutional change, if any is needed, it would be best to make.

I must speak with absolute freedom and candor in this matter, or not speak at all; and it seems to me that the present position of the presidency in our actual system, as we use it, is quite abnormal and must lead eventually to something very different.

He is expected by the Nation to be the leader of his party as well as the chief executive officer of the Government, and the country will take no excuses from him. He must play the part and play it successfully or lose the country's confidence. He must be prime minister, as much concerned with the guidance of legislation as with the just and orderly execution of law, and he is the spokesman of the Nation in everything, even the most momentous and most delicate dealings of the Government with foreign nations.

Why in such circumstances should he be responsible to no one for four long years? All the people's legislative spokesmen in the House of Representatives and one-third of their representatives in the Senate are brought to book every two years; why not the President, if he is to be the leader of the party and the spokesman of policy?

Sooner or later, it would seem, he must be made answerable to opinion in a somewhat more informal and intimate fashion—answerable, it may be, to the Houses whom he seeks to lead, either personally or through a Cabinet, as well as to the people for whom they speak. But that is a matter to be worked out—as it inevitably will be—in some natural American way which we cannot yet even predict.

The present fact is that the President is held responsible for what happens in Washington in every large matter, and so long as he is commanded to lead he is surely entitled to a certain amount of power—all the power he can get from the support and convictions and opinions of his fellow countrymen; and he ought to be suffered to use that power against his opponents until his work is done. It will be very difficult for him to abuse it. He holds it upon sufferance, at the pleasure of public opinion. Everyone else, his opponents included, has access to opinion, as he has. He must keep the confidence of the country by earning it, for he can keep it in no other way.

Put the present customary limitation of two terms into the Constitution, if you do not trust the people to take care of themselves, but make it two terms (not one, because four years is often too long), and give the President a chance to win the full service by proving himself fit for it.

If you wish to learn the result of Constitutional ineligibility to reelection, ask any former governor of New Jersey, for example, what the effect is in actual experience. He will tell you how cynically and with what complacence the politicians banded against him waited for the inevitable end of his term to take their chances with his successor.

Constitutions place and can place no limitations upon their power. They may control what governors they can as long as they please, as long as they can keep their outside power and influence together. They smile at the coming and going of governors as some men in Washington have smiled at the coming and going of Presidents, as upon things ephemeral which passed and were soon enough got rid of if you but sat tight and waited.

As things stand now the people might more likely be cheated than served by further limitations of the President's eligibility. His fighting power in their behalf would be immensely weakened. No one will fear a President except those whom he can make fear the elections.

We singularly belie our own principles by seeking to determine by fixed Constitutional provision what the people shall determine for themselves and are perfectly competent to determine for themselves. We cast a doubt upon the whole theory of popular Government.

I believe that we should fatally embarrass ourselves if we made the Constitutional change proposed. If we want our Presidents to fight our battles for us, we should give them the means, the legitimate means, the means their opponents will always have. Strip them of everything else but the right to appeal to the people, but leave them that; suffer them to be leaders; absolutely prevent them from being bosses. . . .

I am very well aware that my position on this question will be misconstrued, but that is a matter of perfect indifference to me. The truth is much more important than my reputation for modesty and lack of personal ambition. My reputation will take care of itself, but Constitutional questions and questions of policy will not take care of themselves without frank and fearless discussion.

Franklin Delano Roosevelt: President of the United States, March 4, 1933–

Address to Democratic Victory Dinner, March 4, 1937: My great ambition on January 20, 1941, is to turn over this desk and chair in the White House to my successor, whoever he may be, with the assurance that I am at the same time turning over to him as President, a Nation intact, a Nation at peace, a Nation prosperous, a Nation clear in its knowledge of what powers it has to serve its own citizens, a Nation that is in a position to use those powers to the full in order to move forward steadily to meet the modern needs of humanity—a Nation which has thus proved that the democratic form and methods of national government can and will succeed.

Presidents Should Be Limited to One Term

John D. Works

In the following viewpoint, John D. Works, a Republican U.S. senator from California from 1911 to 1917, contends that a single term is better for the presidency and the country as a whole than two terms would be, as the president would not have to waste time and energy campaigning for a second term and could instead deal with the issues facing the country. Works had proposed a Senate resolution to amend the U.S. Constitution, limiting the president to a single six-year term. He argues in this 1912 speech before the Senate that a campaigning president is undignified and represents an inappropriate use of presidential power.

I am not urging this amendment to the Constitution because of the length of time a President may serve, but to prevent his holding a second term, with all the evils resulting from the use of patronage to secure a renomination and re-election. I would not object to the holding of a second term if such term did not follow immediately after the first. I would rather—much rather—see one term of ten years than two terms of four years each in immediate succession.

This movement to bring about the amendment of the Constitution is not the result of a sudden impulse. It is not a personal matter. It has no connection with the coming political campaign. It is intended to correct a great evil that has grown up under the Constitution as it now is and which is growing with every political campaign. If this change were made, the American people would be spared the humiliating spectacle of a President of the United States traveling up and

John D. Works, "The Question of Changing the President's Term of Office," in *Congressional Digest*, May 1938, vol. 17, no. 5, pp. 149–60.

down the country, guarded by an Army officer and private detectives, making political speeches and urging his own reelection. The White House would not be turned into a political press gallery, managed by the Secretary of the President. The official head of this great Nation would be free from the overpowering temptation to use his office and his power as such to secure a second term. Time was when such efforts to secure the great office of President of the United States was looked upon as a disgrace to the Nation and unworthy of a candidate therefor.

It was an unfortunate day for this country when one of its distinguished, honorable, and well-beloved citizens inaugurated the system, as a candidate for President, of receiving delegates at his home and discussing political questions, ostensibly for their information but, in fact, to be sent broadcast throughout the country. That was the beginning of an evil and wholly inexcusable custom, by which the great office of President of the United States was brought down to the level of self-seeking politics and personal appeals for office. Now, and for a long time, the candidate does not wait for delegations to come to him. He goes out on the stump and discusses political questions, abuses his opponents, and urges the continuance in power of his party, involving his own reelection. To me it is a pitiful and humiliating spectacle. Who does a President represent in his official capacity during his term of office? Presumably the whole people of the country of every political faith and shade of belief. But does he, in fact, under present conditions? No, he does not. The President has come to be regarded as the head of his political party. Instead of laying aside politics and assuming the position of representative of the people, he becomes, if he had not been so before, a politician, the titular head and leader of his party, with all that that implies. And what does it imply and what follows? Every appointee of his, from the highest to the lowest office, considers that he owes him not official loyalty alone, but political and personal loyalty as well. He seems to feel that he must support the President in his political views and aspirations, personal and otherwise, even to supporting him for reelection, or get out of office. Few of them choose the latter course.

The evils of such a system are too obvious to need comment. Every thinking man sees and knows the evils of it; but what are we doing to prevent it? One President may very well say, in his justification, or by way of excuse, for nothing can justify it: 'Other Presidents have done it before me. It is the custom. Why should I not secure a second term by such means as my predecessors have done?' I have lived in hopes that some time we would elect a Chief Magistrate of this Republic with moral courage and determination enough to put this pernicious and obnoxious custom under his feet. I have been disappointed. I realize that the temptation to follow the custom, and thus secure a reelection, is a tremendous temptation. So far it has been an overpowering one.

Allegiance to the President

Let us look for a moment at the consequences, or some or them, that flow from this condition of things. The President has the power to appoint thousands of public officers. They are found in every city, town, and village in the country. Every one of these appointees, from a Cabinet officer down, with very rare exceptions, considers himself as owing political allegiance to the President personally. In fact, with most of them, this personal political allegiance is looked upon as far more binding than their official obligation to the public. When the Presidential term of office is about to expire you will find them all from the highest to the lowest lined up for him and supporting him for a second term. If they are capable of it they take the stump in his behalf. If not stump orators they belong to the gumshoe brigade that works so effectually with the individual voter. The question of his fitness for a second term or his convictions on fundamental governmental ques-

Election campaign poster for President Franklin D. Roosevelt's third term, which began in 1941. He was the only American president to serve four consecutive terms. Election Campaign Poster featuring President Franklin D. Roosevelt, 1941 (color litho), American School, (20th century) / Private Collection / Peter Newark American Pictures / The Bridgeman Art Library.

tions has no weight with them. He is their political chief, as they understand, and their support is his absolute right. But there is another consideration of no little weight with the President's appointees. If he is not reelected they will lose their jobs and thereby the country be deprived of their most valuable services. Does anyone believe that the people of this country are satisfied with this condition? Certainly they are not. They do not believe in it. It is a custom that has been under public censure and condemnation from the time it was inaugurated.

It is not alone that such a system enables the President to build up a good political machine, with representatives in every county of every state of the Union, through which he may force his renomination, that it meets with public commendation, but because it imposes a burden upon the presidential office that it should not bear. Why should the President be burdened with the appointment of the thousands of Federal officials now subject to his choice? Why should not these appointments be placed under the classified Civil Service rules and made to stand upon merit and not on political or personal favors of Senators or anyone else?

The proposed amendment to the Constitution that I have offered would, if adopted, take away from the President every opportunity or temptation to strive for his own reelection or to use the power or influence of the thousands of his appointees to secure his reelection or the success of his party.

I am not wedded to any particular term for the President, long or short, as I have said the length of term is not the important matter to be considered. It is the right of the President under the present rule to succeed himself that I am combating.

I would have no objection to four years or eight years as the term of office. I would not be willing to go beyond eight years. What I desire to impress upon the Senate is my unutterable objection to two terms, one following the other. I do not believe in changing the Constitution except for grave reasons affecting the public interests. I am particularly averse to any changes affecting the fundamental principles of government. But I consider the change I am seeking to bring about as one of profound interest and grave consequence. It will not change the principles established by the Constitution, principles that we should be careful to preserve and maintain, or invade fundamental questions. It simply destroys the condition that has afforded an opportunity to build up a vicious political system that every good citizen should deplore.

What the Public Thinks About Presidential Tenure

Daniel Starch

In this viewpoint, from a poll that appeared in the Washington
Star *newspaper in 1936, Daniel Starch asked Americans whether
they favored a single six-year term over a four-year term with
the option for reelection for the U.S. presidency. The majority of
those polled—66.4 percent—did not favor a six-year term, while
26.7 percent did favor it. More than 25 percent of those who favored the four-year term said that six years was too long to test
the competency of the president, especially if the president were
doing an unsatisfactory job. Others in the majority group felt
that a four-year term was more democratic because giving the
American people more frequent chances to cast a vote for president would keep the administration more sensitive to public
opinion. Of those who favored a six-year term, many thought
that without reelection in mind, the president would be more effective at dealing with the issues of the country. The question of
presidential tenure was prevalent in November 1936, as Franklin
Delano Roosevelt had just won a second term in a landslide victory over Republican candidate Alf Landon and much discussion
revolved around Roosevelt running for an unprecedented third
term.*

*Starch, a psychologist as well as a business administration
professor, developed business research tools such as polls and
readership surveys.*

If a Constitutional Amendment were to be proposed limiting the President of the United States to a single six-year
term, it would receive the support of little more than a quarter of the people.

Daniel Starch, "The Starch Commercial Research Poll—1936," *Washington Star*, November 29, 1936.

This is the conclusion from a polling America survey of sentiment on the question, "Do you favor a single six-year term for the President instead of the present tenure?" Opinions were divided as follows:

Yes	26.7%
No	66.4
No opinion	6.9
	100.0%

The question of presidential tenure has been of more than ordinary current interest. It was emphasized by the attitude taken by a large proportion of those who voted a second term for Mr. [Franklin D.] Roosevelt, who said that he needed another term to carry out the program which he had started in his first four years but had not had time to complete.

The Roosevelt landslide provoked discussion of whether or not the President would seek a third term. The Constitution places no limit upon the number of terms a President may serve, but [George] Washington's refusal of a third term set a precedent which has always been followed.

A proposal to limit the office to a single term was included in the Democratic platform adopted at the Baltimore convention in 1912. This convention, which nominated Woodrow Wilson for President, contained the plank: "We favor a single presidential term and to that end urge the adoption of an amendment to the Constitution making the President of the United States ineligible for reelection, and we pledge the candidate of this convention to this principle."

A Single Six-Year Term

The proposal for a single six-year term for the President is being included in a group of electoral reforms for which sponsorship is being urged by Senator [George W.] Norris of Nebraska. These also include direct election of the President and Vice-President and division of each State's electoral vote in accordance with the popular suffrage.

Of those who favored a single six-year term, 41.8 per cent said they thought the President would be able to do a better job if he did not have to think of reelection. The effect of the campaign for reelection was expressed by a roofing salesman: "If a President was serving for only one term, he could enforce the policies he thought best without being always compelled to do the bidding of various groups of voters with selfish interests." A student put it: "With campaigning in the fourth year, the President's term is really three years long, which isn't long enough to carry out national programs."

Among many persons there was the feeling that a President of the United States takes from the duties attendant his office not only time for campaigning for reelection, but a great deal of time throughout his term to build up his party machine; they feel that an unduly large proportion of the persons with whom he talks come to see him not on public business, but to ask private favors. "A longer term would enable the President to spend an adequate amount of time to work out plans for the Nation, rather than worrying about his political machine and reelection," maintained a book salesman in Indianapolis.

"A six-year term gives the President security in office—he would not have to play politics all during the term," declared a physician. A designer of castings had the same reaction: "As it is now, the President spends his first term trying to get himself elected to a second term, instead of looking after the best interests of all the people."

The group which thought that four years is too short a term to accomplish a program was almost as large as the preceding group; it comprised 35.6 per cent of those who favored the six-year term. They all felt that a national program, especially if it is a program which is initiated by a new administration and is not merely a continuation of the policies of the same party, is a complicated business which requires more than four years to develop.

This 1940 political cartoon depicting President Franklin D. Roosevelt as an Egyptian Sphinx alludes to the controversy surrounding his election to a third term.

"The administration in power should have the opportunity to work out its ideas adequately before the people are asked to judge them," said a Boston secretary. A lawyer thought: "It takes that long for the President to get his teeth in the situation." One housewife declared that four years was not long enough to accomplish any national program. Many others agreed that during six years of uninterrupted effort an

63

administration should be able to begin and complete a program, but that this could hardly be done during a four-year term, the last year of which was largely taken up by efforts to be reelected.

There was a sharp drop in the number of persons who comprised the next group; they said that the elimination of the campaign for a second four-year term would mean less mud-slinging, less political uncertainty and less distraction to the people generally. This group constituted 14.5 per cent of those favoring the six-year term.

While it was realized that any national election would cause a certain amount of uncertainty, these people said that there would be less of this with elections every six years. "These elections keep the country disrupted all the time," complained one housewife. Another suggested, "Two new men up each six years would obviate all the mud-slinging against the President's last administration."

There was 13.7 per cent of this group who approved a single term because it would reduce campaign expenses. Impressed by the amounts said to have been spent on the election just passed, many people said this money was largely wasted, and the less frequently it was necessary to have expensive campaigns the better for the national income.

Smaller groups said that the eight years permissible now was too long a term. Said a Dallas lawyer, "I voted for Roosevelt, but I'd feel better if he was going to be in office only two more years."

Why a Four-Year Term Is Better

Of the great majority who favored the present tenure for the presidency about a third looked at the progress which America has made in the past and concluded that the present tenure had proved satisfactory. "It has always worked well," or "it has worked out all right so far," asserted a great many persons.

Public Opinion of a Two-Term Limit for the Office of the President

Date	Percent for Two-Term Limit	Percent Against
June 1936	57	43
1937	49	51
1938	48	52
1939	42	58
1940	41	59
1943 (April)	46	54
1943 (Dec.)	54	46
1944 (April)	57	43
1945 (May)	60	40
1947 (Feb.)	57	43
1947 (May)	59	41

TAKEN FROM: *Public Opinion Quarterly*, vol. 2, 1947–1948, pp. 304–305.

Others gave more specific reasons for their satisfaction. A Hoosier [Indiana resident] declared, "If the President isn't any good, we can get rid of him sooner under the present system. On the other hand, a good President can be put in office for four more years." The operator of a boys' camp maintained, "Four years is long enough for an inefficient man, but eight years is not long enough for a good one, like the one we have now."

Precedent weighed heavily with persons who said, "Let well enough alone," or "I believe we should be ruled by precedent." But the great bulk of the persons in this class favored the present tenure because it makes it easier to effect a change if a change is found desirable, whereas it guarantees a good President an adequate tenure.

More than 25 per cent of the group which favored the present tenure said that six years is too long a term if the

President proves to be unsatisfactory. A Los Angeles lawyer said, "Under the six-year system it is just too bad if the man turns out to be a poor President." A Southern housewife put it, "Six years is too long if the wrong man gets in and not long enough if a good man like Roosevelt gets in." A machinist declared, "Often a President does not live up to his expectations. Under the present system we can get him out of office at the end of four and not six years."

"If we get a crook or a bonehead in office we don't want to be forced to have to keep him six years. We've just proved that a good man can be reelected," answered a Texan. This point of view was repeated in many, many ways, such as "Four years is long enough for a poor President," or "If we should get a President who is not doing the right thing it would be better to get rid of him at the end of four years than at the end of six."

The third largest group among those who favored the present tenure was comprised of those who said that four years is long enough to test the ability of a President, so that he may be reelected if he has proved satisfactory. The manager of a dress shop summed up this attitude. "Four years gives the people a fair chance to learn what the President can do. If he's good they'll reelect him, if not they'll defeat him." A bookkeeper said, "Four years gives a man sufficient chance to show if he's good without giving him time to do too much damage if he's not." A wholesaler of women's hats contended, "Six years is too long a time to have a dangerous man in the presidential chair. It is better to have a trial period of four years and then get rid of him if he bungles things—or leave him in for another term if he's dependable."

Preserving the Democracy

Of these persons who favored the present tenure, 6.5 per cent said they did so because it is more democratic. They said that it gives the people more frequent opportunities to register their approval or disapproval of a Chief Executive and that it therefore keeps the administration more sensitive to public opinion.

There was some fear of dictatorship expressed. Some thought that a strong President, with dictatorial tendencies, could become too firmly entrenched for the Nation's good in six years. A nurse maintained, "A President would get to feel that a crown should go with the position."

While there were some who maintained that a six-year term was preferable because they felt four years was too brief a period, there were others, and they constituted 5.4 per cent of those opposed to the longer tenure, who maintained that a term of six years was too short a period to institute and complete a program. They emphasized that if the electorate approved of an administration's program at the end of four years, they could return this administration to complete its work.

Closely allied to this argument was the notion expressed by a small percentage that elections every four years had a good effect on administrations in that they provided helpful checks, and that if the President was returned to office he would feel encouraged to proceed with the same policies he had adopted more tentatively in his first term.

Other small groups asserted that an election every four years meant a more frequent alteration of parties in power, and that this was beneficial to the Nation; that to change the present system would mean amending the Constitution, and they were opposed to that; and that more frequent elections tended to reduce graft in the Federal administration and to stimulate business.

The 6.9 per cent who were undecided or had no opinion said in some cases that it made no difference whether the term was six or four, and in others that they were inclined to favor a four-year term with no reelection.

On several polling America studies where a "yes" or "no" question has been asked, the undecided group has amounted to about 7 per cent, suggesting that about that proportion of the population either is so uninformed on questions of current interest that it cannot express an opinion or else is congenitally unable to make up its mind.

Amendment XXII Is Necessary for Democracy

The New York Times

In the following viewpoint, a 1951 editorial from The New York Times, *the author argues that Amendment XXII is necessary to keep a rotation of office. This editorial, which ran just weeks after the states ratified the Twenty-second Amendment to the Constitution, expresses the author's glad sentiments that an amendment establishing term limits for the presidency has been approved. The author raises the issue of national security in times of emergency when a new president is to take office. According to the author, it is the responsibility of the incumbent president to develop someone within his own administration or party to take over the leadership role. This will assure the public of a stable force in the country's leadership and will maintain continuity in the Oval Office without one individual usurping the power of the presidency.*

The New York Times, *established in 1851, is the nation's largest metropolitan newspaper.*

A sudden rush of activity on the part of the state Legislatures has added a new Amendment to the Constitution of the United States. This is the Twenty-second Amendment, which declares that after Mr. [Harry] Truman (who is specifically exempted) no President shall be elected for more than two terms, or elected more than once if he has served in excess of two years of his predecessor's term. The Amendment was approved by Congress and referred to the states in the spring of 1947. The first eighteen of the necessary thirty-six ratifications by the states were obtained that year. Only six ad-

This 1895 political cartoon depicts President Grover Cleveland as the ancient Greek mythological character of Narcissus, who was bewitched by the beauty of his own image. Here, Cleveland is enamored with his own third-term ambition. The Art Archive/ The Picture Desk, Inc.

ditional states added their ratifications in the three succeeding years. But twelve states have voted favorably within the last few weeks, and with their approval the Amendment now becomes a part of the basic law of the United States.

The strongest argument made against the Amendment at the time of its adoption by Congress was that it might tie the hands of the electorate in some grave future national emergency and prevent the voters from exercising a free choice in their own best interest. Undoubtedly this argument had considerable force. The nation might find itself in a state of war, or approaching a state of war, when the second term of a President in office expired, and the case for continuing that President in office could be very strong indeed. Such a situation did arise, in fact, in 1940, and again (after a third term) in 1944.

Good Policies Can Continue

The persuasive answer to this argument is that, with the new Amendment in force, any President who happens to be in office when such an emergency arises will henceforth find it necessary, and will surely find it possible, to do what Mr. [Franklin Delano] Roosevelt failed to do in 1940 and 1944—namely, develop within his own Administration, or elsewhere within his party, an alternative leadership to his own, fully capable of presenting his policies adequately to the electorate. In such circumstances, the voters, if they so desired, would be able to achieve a continuity of policy in the White House.

For the rest: the strong arguments which established the century-and-a-half-old tradition against a third term still prevail, and have gained increasing force from the fact of the enormously larger powers of the Presidency and the obvious hazards of too-long-continued centralization of these powers in the hands of any individual, however worthy. We welcome the adoption of the Amendment.

A National Committee Opposes Amendment XXII

Bernard Lemelin

In the following viewpoint, Bernard Lemelin examines the arguments of the National Committee Against Limiting the Presidency in opposition to the Twenty-second Amendment to the Constitution. This group, which opposed the passage of Amendment XXII, was founded in 1949 by journalist Daniel Francis Clancy. Clancy and other committee members—including Harold L. Ickes, Franklin Delano Roosevelt's interior secretary; Maury Maverick, a Texas lawyer and member of Congress; and Joseph F. Guffey, a former U.S. senator from Pennsylvania—believed that an amendment limiting the tenure of the president was undemocratic and a serious blow to the freedom and liberty of the American people. The National Committee Against Limiting the Presidency argued that the Constitution should be left unchanged regarding this matter and that the people of the United States should be trusted enough to decide how long they want a president to remain in office. Lemelin is a history professor at Laval University in Quebec City, Canada.

O n March 24, 1947, as a posthumous slap at Franklin Delano Roosevelt and his unprecedented four terms in the White House, the Republicans of the 80th Congress passed the Twenty-second Amendment to the Constitution limiting presidents to two terms. With the ratification by a 36th state (Nevada), it finally became law on February 26, 1951. According to Massachusetts Congressman Joseph Martin of the Grand Old Party [Republicans], this landmark event represented nothing less than a "victory for the people and their republican form of Government [and] a defeat for totalitari-

Bernard Lemelin, "Opposition to the 22nd Amendment," *Canadian Review of American Studies*, vol. 29, 1999, p. 133. Copyright © Canadian Review of American Studies 1999. Reprinted by permission of the publisher.

anism and the enemies of freedom." For his part, Harry S. Truman, after his presidency, vehemently opposed such an amendment, describing it as . . . "one of the worst that has been put into the Constitution, except for the Prohibition Amendment." In his view, "there are clearly times when more than two terms are both necessary and wise." Among the organizations also critical of this measure, the National Committee Against Limiting the Presidency, founded in 1949, was certainly the most active.

Organized Opposition

Although one cannot provide an exact birthdate for the National Committee Against Limiting the Presidency, we know at least that its founding occurred near the beginning of 1949. Illustrative of this is a letter dated February 12, written by Daniel Francis Clancy, founder of the committee, in which he declared that "in an effort to prevent ratification of the 22nd Amendment . . . I am forming a National Committee against Limiting the Presidency." . . .

More information is available on Clancy's arguments as director of the committee, which was composed of Harold L. Ickes, Franklin D. Roosevelt's interior secretary; Michael Francis Doyle, president of the Electoral Colleges of the United States; Maury Maverick, a Texas lawyer and member of the 74th and 75th Congresses; Joseph F. Guffey, the former U.S. senator from Pennsylvania; C. F. Richards, a Texas attorney; and Edmund C. Gorrell, a newspaper editor from Winamac, Indiana. In a series of letters, Clancy explained why he opposed the Twenty-second Amendment. In one of them, dated April 26, 1949, and sent to Alabama Governor James Folsom, he asserted the need to respect the document that had emerged from the Philadelphia Convention of 1787 and to rely on the American people: "We of this committee are against the amendment, which would limit Presidents to two terms— believing that the Presidency should be left as it was planned in the Constitution, and that the people can be trusted to know how long they want a President." A letter to Harold Ickes dated September 23 of the same year expressed similar arguments and said that "the wise nation will set up no barrier against utilizing ability or exploiting experience." ...

Clancy's primary goal ... was to demonstrate the incongruity of the two contentions upon which the opponents to a third term based their arguments. To the first contention saying that it is foolish to assert that at any one time there is only one man in a nation of 130,000,000 people who is fitted to be Chief Executive, he retorted that "the choice is not one in 130,000,000 but, in nomination, one in six or a dozen and, in election, one in two." Clancy added that he could not give credence to such an assertion, since he deeply believed in the theory of indispensability, "that is, that for certain periods in a nation's political history one man may be better fitted for leadership than any of the other eligible aspirants." As for the second contention which suggested the danger of making self-perpetuation possible through the long-term implementation of powerful bureaucratic mechanisms, he replied "that the real issue involved in the perpetuity in office argument is *party* patronage and not *personal* patronage, since actual obtainment of the office is a matter of election and only party patronage influences elections." Convinced that the tradition of two terms was supported far more by prejudice and partisanship than by sound political philosophy, Clancy concluded ... that long governmental tenure in other democratic countries tended to be without ill effects and was quite common. That was especially true for the United States' northern neighbor, as he contended:

> Turning to the Dominion of Canada ..., we find that four men have held the office of prime minister for longer than eight years—Prime Minister [Robert] Borden for slightly over eight years, Prime Minister [Wilfrid] Laurier for fifteen years, Prime Minister [John A.] MacDonald (1867–73 and

Paul Jacob is an advocate for legislative term limits. Between 1992 and 2007, he served in several capacities in the nonprofit organization U.S. Term Limits (USTL), which lobbies for term limits for elected officials at every level of government. Douglas Graham/ Congressional Quarterly/Getty Images.

1878–91) for nineteen years, and Prime Minister [William Lyon Mackenzie] King (1921–30, excepting a two month interval in 1926, and from 1935 to the present [1940]).

Other members of the National Committee Against Limiting the Presidency echoed Clancy's arguments during the Truman era. For instance, in March 1949, Michael Francis Doyle insisted on the need to honor the Constitution: "It is my belief that this great document should not be changed for temporary or for local reasons. . . . There is no valid reason whatsoever in limiting the Presidency to two terms. Another Congress may want to limit it to one term; others may want to limit it to three terms." That same month, Harold Ickes, who launched a campaign in 1940 in favor of a third term for Roosevelt, deplored what he saw as the lack of faith of the supporters of the Twenty-second Amendment in Congress when he said that "it is really nothing less than sneering impertinence of the politicians to disregard the will of the people as expressed both in 1940 and 1944, and attempt to force on them a limitation of presidential tenure which clearly they do not want." In a letter of February 1951, Truman's former secretary of interior expressed once again the need to remain confident in the American electors: "I am against that amendment as a matter of principle. I believe that the people ought to have the right to choose, for as many terms as they may elect, all of the officers for whom the Constitution gives them the right to vote." In another statement, Ickes evoked the pernicious consequences which might have resulted from an earlier adoption of the Twenty second Amendement: "If the proposed amendment had been in effect in 1940, no one looking back at that critical and fateful period can even imagine the confusion, the utter disunity . . . that might have resulted under some other President, however patriotic and well-intentioned he might have been." He added that "the brilliant conception of lend lease, a law which made it possible for us to keep our allies in the war until we ourselves got ready, of itself justified the reelection of President Roosevelt for a third term."

Was Amendment XXII Inevitable?

In spite of all the activities of the National Committee Against Limiting the Presidency, the Twenty-second Amendment was finally passed in 1951. For many reasons, this result, which was already regretted by scholar Clinton Rossiter in the fifties was to be expected.

First, there was what some observers have characterized as "party rancor and personal hatred" in the post-World War II American political landscape. Indeed, numerous Republicans tended to despise the late Franklin D. Roosevelt. This is understandable since he appeared as the man who had kept the Grand Old Party from power for more than a decade. Many believed, in addition, that the Democratic politician from

Hyde Park [New York], in what they felt was his lust for power, broke in 1940 the two-term tradition inaugurated by George Washington and Thomas Jefferson. Criticizing Roosevelt's action, Senator Kenneth Wherry, a Republican from Nebraska and a vociferous foe of New Deal liberalism, said for instance in 1943:

> The moment the unwritten law was ignored by the occupant of the White House, the way was opened to a life presidency. Such executive tenure is entirely foreign to the fundamental principles of American government. . . . When any incumbent of our highest executive office utterly disregards a precedent established by unwritten law, then we must enact a written restriction to curb insatiable ambitions.

These considerations may explain why historian Arthur Schlesinger, Jr., has characterized the Twenty-second Amendment as primarily a repudiation of Franklin D. Roosevelt. However that may be, if Capitol Hill's Republicans had tried to introduce resolutions during the Second World War to amend the Constitution for limiting any President to two terms, they would have met with an important problem: the pro-Roosevelt New Deal Democrats held a majority in the legislative branch. Nevertheless, the context became less favorable for these Democrats after the November 1946 elections: Republicans were in majority in both houses of Congress. Best known for its assault on New Deal programs and its refusal to consolidate the welfare state, the conservative 80th Congress introduced, as early as January 1947, several resolutions to limit the presidential term of office to eight years. Among them was House Joint Resolution 27, destined to become the Twenty-second Amendment, which was approved by the lower house in February by a vote of 285 to 121 and a few weeks later by the upper house by a vote of 59 to 23. Not surprisingly, all of the Republicans in both houses endorsed this resolution while most Democrats opposed it. Incidentally, Democratic Congressman Adolph Sabath of Illinois was particularly harsh on the Republican supporters of House Resolution 27, qualifying their triumph as a "pitiful victory over a great man now sleeping on the banks of the Hudson." Interestingly enough, Frederick Zucker noted that of the 47 Democratic supporters of the resolution in the lower house, almost all of them were anti-New Dealers and represented southern states.

Influence of Contemporary Events

The passage of the Twenty-second Amendment was all the more inevitable because a slim majority of state legislatures was controlled by the Grand Old Party from 1947 onwards. This was significant as all of the 25 Republican-controlled legislatures ratified the Twenty-second Amendment between 1947 and 1951. Although most of the Democratic state legislatures were opposed to this measure during the same period, they did not present the same degree of unity: all of the southern Democratic legislatures, for instance, voted in favor of the Twenty-second Amendment. Moreover, it must be noted that several influential newspapers such as the *Chicago Tribune*, the *Washington Star* and the *New York Times* took editorial positions for the amendment. The latter newspaper, for instance, said in March 1947 that the proposed amendment should be rapidly ratified, pleading that it would prevent a Chief Executive from building "his personal power to irresistible proportions." In addition, although Truman did not hesitate to attack the Twenty-second Amendment after his presidency, he did not support Clancy's pressure group in 1949–51. As a matter of fact, the incumbent of the White House seemed rather indifferent to the general debate over this amendment, as Frederick Zucker has noted: "Truman would be expected to oppose the amendment as a legislative encroachment designed to weaken a President in his second term. . . . [Nevertheless, he] did not play any active part in the process by which the 22nd Amendment was proposed and ratified. His role was strictly passive." Truman's laconic reaction to the ratification of February 1951 corroborated such a viewpoint. Among the hypotheses which might explain Truman's passivity towards the Twenty-second Amendment was the fact that his Administration faced overwhelming foreign problems in 1949 and especially in 1950 with the outbreak of the Korean conflict. As presidential adviser Clark Clifford said in this respect: "The Korean war changed forever the character of the Truman Administration. Priorities were suddenly reversed, as the nation and its leaders once again had to put a faraway war ahead of domestic need." In short, whatever the reasons underlying Truman's attitude, the Chief Executive hardly provided a stimulus or an inspiration source for members of the National Committee Against Limiting the Presidency.

This particular conjuncture alone, however, was not sufficient to explain the enactment of the Twenty-second Amendment. A structural factor, linked to the fears generated by the vast expansion of the presidency's authority during the Great Depression and especially during the Second World War, must also be taken into account. Indeed, many Americans, after 1945, aware that the presidency was not the only institution, came to believe that Chief Executive's long tenure threatened the separation of powers and the system of checks and balances. Such a belief appeared all the sounder in that the phenomenal growth of presidential powers, in this incipient Cold War context, did not seem to wane with Franklin D. Roosevelt's successor. As historian Donald McCoy has underscored:

[Truman] was able to expand presidential authority as commander in chief and chief diplomat in order to maintain a powerful American presence internationally. . . . [He] had qualms about the costs of mounting military power, but, as he saw it, at stake were the nation's survival and its way of life. Thus he was seldom timid about using his powers. Truman, for example, held that the president could determine when there was a national emergency endowing him with inherent extra powers ...; was not required to give Congress confidential information ...; had "discretionary power" in spending appropriations ...; and could engage in military action when necessary....

The American Fear of Dictatorship

Fearing the dangers of unrestrained executive authority, quite a few Americans argued that a constitutional two-term limit would help rebalance the scales of governmental power in favor of the legislative branch—a "legislative branch" that Truman, during episodes such as the Berlin crisis and the Korean war, tended to ignore. Representative Joseph Martin, who appeared in his capacity as Speaker the driving force behind House Joint Resolution 27, greeted this argument favorably. Congress represented in his view "the people's special instrument of control over their government and their public officials." Naturally, the state legislatures could hardly deny the desirability of such a development, as scholar Louis Koenig has revealed: "In sending the [22nd] amendment to the state legislatures ..., Congress was relying upon bodies endowed with impressive experience in trammeling executive authority.... In fourteen states governors can serve only one term, and in six states not more than two."

On the whole, the atavistic fear of dictatorship, so prevalent in American history and particularly intensified during the post-World War II period with the deterioration of relations between the United States and the Soviet Union, must certainly not be overlooked to understand the enactment of the Twenty-second Amendment. Needless to say, the same was true for what we call the "mythical power" of the two-term tradition. This significant element, for example, largely explains why a Chief Executive such as Theodore Roosevelt, who "loved being President" and who "still had much to accomplish" decided not to run in 1908 for a second full term, as historian Gil Troy has claimed: "Roosevelt's decision to retire in 1909 stemmed from his vision of the presidency and the continuing American fear of power. Although he had been elected only once, he was President for over seven years and did not want to appear to violate George Washington's two-term precedent. The vast power a president wielded obligated him to keep it only for 'a limited time', Roosevelt explained." ...

In short, these [reasons] made the ratification of the Twenty-second Amendment inevitable, a measure that Dwight Eisenhower, the first Chief Executive to feel its impact, did not hesitate in 1956 to qualify as being "not wholly wise."

Partisan Politics Delayed the Ratification of Amendment XXII

Paul G. Willis and George L. Willis

In the following viewpoint, historians Paul G. Willis and George L. Willis provide political background on the ratification of Amendment XXII of the U.S. Constitution, which limits presidential time in office to two four-year terms. The authors explain that House Joint Resolution 27, later to become Amendment XXII, was introduced in the House in January 1947, where it passed on February 5, and was referred to the Senate on February 7. It was accepted on March 24, and was then referred to the state legislatures for ratification. It took many years for the states to ratify it—thanks to partisan politics, Willis and Willis contend. The Democratic Party saw the resolution as a censure of Franklin Delano Roosevelt, since the resolution was introduced toward the end of the New Deal Democrat's unprecedented fourth term as president, which was being served out by Harry Truman after Roosevelt died in office. The Republicans denied this claim, stating that the law was necessary to protect the office of the presidency from becoming a dictatorship, controlled by one person. Because of these political overtones, it took four years for the ratification process to be completed. In early 1951, Amendment XXII was ratified.

On February 27, 1951, the thirty-sixth state ratified the Twenty-second Amendment. Thus ended efforts made since 1789 to fill in the omission left in the Constitution by the framers concerning presidential re-eligibility. Undoubtedly party rancor and personal hatred were among the factors that contributed to the proposal and ratification of the amendment. But there were more substantial stakes involved. The

Paul G. Willis and George L. Willis, "The Politics of the Twenty-Second Amendment," *The Western Political Quarterly*, vol. 5, September 1952, pp. 469–82.

presidency is today the chief institution in our government. But it is not the only institution. Political forces express themselves through institutions. Some forces find one institution, some another, amenable to manipulation. Without undue oversimplification it may be said that the presidency has proved to be the vehicle most appropriate for the nationalizing, centralizing, and unifying forces in our society; the Congress, the states, and the local party organizations have been most susceptible to local, particular, and fragmentizing forces. The Twenty-second Amendment was a victory, which however in the nature of things can hardly be a final victory, of the divisive over the unifying.

The *Federalist* attests that the potentialities of the presidency were in some degree foreseen at the time of the adoption of the Constitution. Prohibition of re-election was even then considered as a device for limiting the presidency. George Washington's refusal of a third term, erected into a political principle by the example of Thomas Jefferson, established a two-term tradition. From [Andrew] Jackson to [Abraham] Lincoln a one-term tradition flourished, and was quite candidly justified as an expression of the Whig philosophy of legislative supremacy. Lincoln broke with tradition and his re-election restored the two-term tradition, which enjoyed a precarious life until 1940.

Attempts to Limit Presidential Tenure

Those who had an interest in applying limits to presidential tenure were never satisfied with the force of tradition. Between 1789 and 1947 no less than 270 resolutions to limit eligibility for re-election were introduced in Congress. Moreover, the frequency of such proposals increased sharply after 1900. It seems safe to say that these proposals reflect something more than concern over tenure. They reflect concern over the presidency itself; they were attacks upon the institution at the only point at which there seemed to be a prospect of success. . . .

It is against [a background of partisan politics] that the breach made in the two-term tradition by Franklin Roosevelt's third and fourth elections in 1940 and 1944 must be viewed. It is as one interlude in this protracted struggle that the adoption of the Twenty-second Amendment must be interpreted.

House Joint Resolution 27, destined to become the Twenty-second Amendment to the Constitution, was introduced in the House on January 3, 1947, by Representative Earl C. Michener and was referred to the Committee on the Judiciary. It was reported favorably to the House on February 5. The next day, after two hours of debate, the joint resolution was passed by a vote of 285-121, with twenty-six recorded as not voting.

In the Senate, where the proposal was received on February 7, it was referred to the Committee on the Judiciary. On February 21, the measure was reported out of the committee by Senator Alexander Wiley with the recommendation that it be passed. Debate on the joint resolution in the Senate was sandwiched in with other business of that house on March 3, 7, 10, and 12, when it was passed by a vote of 59-23, with thirteen not voting. Amendments added in the Senate to the House version of the proposal caused the appointment of a conference committee in the Senate. This committee was not required to function, however, because the joint resolution, as amended in the Senate and returned to the House on March 13, was accepted by the latter body on March 21. The House Committee on House Administration filed House Joint Resolution 27 with the Secretary of State on March 24 for transmittal to the state legislatures. No public hearings were held.

Republicans vs. Democrats

Party faced party in this controversy. The break made in the two-term limitation opened the way to unlimited tenure. By implication, another channel was formed through which cen-

State Ratification of Amendment XXII

Three-quarters of the states must ratify an amendment before it becomes constitutional. Amendment XXII was proposed on March 21, 1947, and when Minnesota ratified it on February 27, 1951, that requirement was fulfilled.

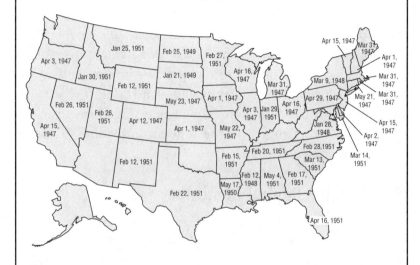

TAKEN FROM: "Ratification of Constitutional Amendments," The U.S. Constitution Online. http://www.usconstitution.net.

tralizing political tendencies could move. Such a development excited the institutional defenders of political decentralization. Under these circumstances, the Republican party, "spiritual heir to the old Whig Party," and enjoying the majority party role in Congress for the first time in over fifteen years, sponsored the limiting joint resolution. The heart of the *stated* Republican position in both houses was contained in the Report recommending adoption of the joint resolution made by the House Judiciary Committee on February 5. . . .

To the Republicans' denial that their measure was a "political question," Democrats charged that it was "anti-Roosevelt" and was inspired by partisan political considerations. Whether for party or for principle, not a single Republican is recorded as having voted against the measure when it passed the House. This performance was repeated in the Senate. The majority of the Democrats in both houses opposed passage of the resolution.

Competition between the parties for the role of champion of "the people" was spirited. Republicans insisted that overthrow of the two-term "precedent" exposed "the people" to a dangerous loss of freedom and possible totalitarianism. Furthermore, a man permitted too long a stay in office stifled the growth of alternative leadership, thus frustrating the electorate. Faced with this situation, "the people should be given the opportunity to set limits on the time an individual can serve as Chief Executive."

"The People" Control Democracy

The reply given by Democratic members was that "the people" "by a mere majority vote, have the opportunity of deciding every four years whether they want to terminate the services of the President if he stands for re-election." "The people" had decided the whole question of presidential tenure on two separate occasions, 1940 and 1944. Hence the proposed limitation would, if adopted, fasten a restriction upon "the people," prohibiting them from retaining in office for more than two terms a president they desired. This, Senator [Scott W.] Lucas thought, "really looks down the road toward dictatorship," since, in an "atomic emergency" and forced to forego, because of this limitation, a leadership they preferred, "the people" might resort to extra-constitutional means to insure a continuation of the leadership they wanted. In any event, the proposed amendment created a constitutional rigidity which later generations might find severely damaging. The proposed restriction, Democrats continued, instead of extending democratic government, moved backward. In a democratic society, "the man elected and the number of times he is elected or reelected comes under the heading of the people's business." This is all the more appropriate since the people are more to be trusted "than a politically minded Congress and some meek State legislatures." How, asked Representative John Lyle, can the limitation which Congress and the state legislatures would fasten on the people by this joint resolution be reconciled with "the supremacy of the people"?

During this part of the debate, however, at least two legislators expressed open distrust of "the people." Representative Kenneth Keating declared that "the threat to our democratic processes from the abuses of autocracy and, therefore, the consummate evil in permitting complete freedom of choice to designate the same person for this office again and again transcends in importance and seriousness what I am also prepared to concede is an evil in limiting the freedom of choice of a free people." In the Senate, Senator Millard Tydings observed that "the people ought to have the right to elect a man to two full terms, . . . and we ought not to deny them the right to elect a President for two full terms, but we ought to provide that a man cannot be elected President for more than two terms."

Democrats questioned the assertion that a "general public discussion" of the problem was in progress. Senator Lucas pointed to the lack of congressional mail on the subject, saying that he had received but "eight pieces of mail" about it. Senator Lister Hill insisted that there was "no demand from the people" for the proposal, as indicated by the fact that he had received "no letter, no telegram, no telephone call, not one word from anyone, about such a constitutional amendment." Other Democrats echoed this sentiment. The tenor of the argument on this point suggests the presence of tacit agreement that, essentially, the controversy was the private concern of opposing party hierarchies. The tight party lines noted when votes were taken seem further to suggest this.

Separation of Powers Threatened

The supporters of the resolution pointed to the danger to legislative supremacy posed by the breach of the two-term tradition. From the point of view of Congress, unlimited presidential tenure signified the end of an advantage traditionally enjoyed by the legislature. Escorted by broad tendencies toward centralization, both in governmental and in party affairs, this change assumed an ominous appearance. Congressional awareness of the issue is reflected in the debates which swirled around House Joint Resolution 27.

Long tenure, it was urged, threatens separation of powers and the check and balance system. The executive could now make the legislature a subservient instrument of his will. Consequently, with the eclipse of their chief protector, the legislature, the people are left exposed and alone before the dangers of unrestrained executive authority, since even the judiciary is threatened. The guardianship of popular rights supplied by the states is likewise affected.

On March 7 a joint resolution was offered in the Senate by Senator [W. Lee] O'Daniel as a substitute for House Joint Resolution 27. It fixed the maximum tenure of all elected federal officers at six years and precluded re-election. Devotion to the high principles announced in the debates above was demonstrated by the margin of defeat, 82-1 (twelve not voting), it suffered.

As was indicated above, the conflict generated by the impact of pressures enforcing centralization upon those directed toward decentralization and localism takes place *within* parties as well as between parties. Centralizing tendencies are stimulated by the presence of unlimited presidential tenure. It is to be expected, then, that the local-state-Congress party alliance, defenders of decentralization, would be excited into a renewed effort to neutralize, if possible to nullify, the advantage thus placed in the hands of the opposition. So, too, because of having experienced a sharper awareness of presidential party potentialities during recent years and thus made more sensitive to their insistent prodding, the conduct of the Democrat party members, on this occasion, might be expected to expose this conflict to clearer view.

President as Party Leader

The rising chorus of intra-party opposition to national party leadership, as it is related to the question of presidential tenure, began as early as 1939. Appearing before a Senate subcommittee in 1940, Thomas J. Coolidge pointed out that President and Congress had not remained separate, as originally intended by the Constitution's makers, because the President had become the leader of his party. "A tremendous power," Coolidge reminded the senators, "is put in his hands over local and national elected Representatives who desire funds for their districts and even over their ability to be reelected. In addition millions of men receive their livelihood at the hands of Presidential appointees." Former Indiana Congressman S. B. Pettengill supported this appraisal, as did other political leaders and former officeholders.

On June 3, 1943, Senator Josiah Bailey introduced another such joint resolution, a move intended, it was said, to discourage President Roosevelt from seeking a fourth term.

A hail of these proposals appeared in Congress following the 1944 election. These were the occasion for the second and last public hearings held on the subject prior to the passage of House Joint Resolution 27. A procession of senators appeared before the subcommittee which conducted this hearing. Each expressed the belief that presidential control of patronage accruing from long tenure threatened to dislocate local-state-Congress party control. Senator [Wayne] Morse did not want to see, in the Republican party, "the party organization that is bound to develop around a man continuing for more than two terms." The discipline applied to Congress which such national party control implied, in regard to both policy direction and elections, did not escape their attention.

Thus, by the time the battle over presidential tenure was renewed again in the 80th Congress, the intra-party differences were sharply defined. The positions taken by members of the House Judiciary Committee reflect these. The Committee was composed of fifteen Republicans and twelve Democrats. While there is no evidence to indicate that a single Republican opposed House Joint Resolution 27 while it was being considered in committee, at least five of the twelve Democrat members supported it. This conflict was further exposed by the appearance of three separate minority views attached to the Committee's Report. Two of these proposed the application of an extreme restriction on presidential tenure. The third opposed any limitation. These three expressions merit closer examination.

The first of the minority views was written by Representative [Emanuel] Celler. Those for whom he spoke took the position that "if there is to be any change in Presidential tenure it should be in the nature of a six-year term, with no right of reelection. . . ."

The second minority view proposed dropping the same noose around presidential tenure, since "the fixing of the tenure of the President . . . at one term of six years would eliminate, *as far as it is possible so to do*, political considerations from the execution of office."

The advantages given to local-state-Congress party control by hobbling the President with one six-year term and prohibiting re-election are obvious. The presidency is thereby made politically impotent. Undiluted congressional control of policy-making is guaranteed. The long-practiced custom of parceling out patronage to decentralized and undisciplined local party claimants is protected. Management of nominating conventions remains in their hands, intact.

The third minority view expressed opposition to both the majority and the two minority attitudes. The six supporters of this last position could not "subscribe to the idea that anything has occurred which justifies the belief that the restrictions upon the rights of the people are necessary." "What," they asked, "have the American people done to justify this restriction being placed upon the democratic process? ... By this amendment we say quite frankly that the people of this great Nation have not sufficient intelligence or judgment to know their own minds, cannot think for themselves, and, as a result we must, therefore, place them in a strait-jacket."

Republicans Push Through Amendment

When House Joint Resolution 27 was voted on in the House on February 6, forty-seven Democrats deserted their party to support the measure. This number indicates that the Democratic deviation of nearly 50 per cent found in committee dwindled to 25 per cent of the party's total House strength when the concealing obscurity of the committee-room was removed.

On the Senate side, the outlines of the intra-party rivalry are less distinct. We do have, however, the word of committee Chairman Wiley that after the Judiciary Committee accepted Amendment No. 2, only one member of the Committee opposed the joint resolution as it was reported. We know, too, that on every recorded vote on amendments, with two exceptions, Republican ranks held firm. No minority views were attached to the Senate Committee's Report. The vote on final passage shows that thirteen Democrats (approximately 25 percent) joined the Republicans, not one of whom bolted his party. This is not to say that the Republican party in Congress did not feel the thrust of intra-party tensions in this matter. It is to say, however, that the requirements of newly acquired power in the legislature, reinforced by the historically conservative party position, did not permit its membership, *at that time*, the luxury of openly-expressed dissensions.

The process of ratification carried on during the next four years exhibits strong political overtones. In March, 1947, when the joint resolution was submitted to the states, twenty-seven state legislatures were in session or thereafter convened. Of these, eighteen ratified the amendment. The fortunes of the Democrats were declining in the early part of 1947. The next year, one in which Democrats elected a president and a congressional majority, only three states ratified the amendment. During the two years which followed only the Dakotas (1949) and Louisiana (1950) ratified it. Then, early in 1951, reflecting the Republican upsurge shown in the congressional elections of the previous November, twelve states, in quick succession, ratified the amendment.

Attaching this provision to the federal Constitution added one more chapter to the history of the search for effective national political leadership.

CONSTITUTIONAL
AMENDMENTS
BEYOND THE BILL OF RIGHTS

CHAPTER 2

Issues Related to Term Limits

The Pros and Cons of a Single Six-Year Presidential Term

Mike Mansfield and Clark M. Clifford

The following viewpoint includes arguments before the 1971 Subcommittee on Constitutional Amendments of the Senate Committee on the Judiciary regarding the subject of a proposed constitutional amendment to establish a single six-year presidential term. Senate majority leader Mike Mansfield, a Democrat from Montana, argues that a single six-year term is more beneficial than two four-year terms because it allows a significant amount of time for the president to set an agenda and frees him from worries about spending time and energy to run a reelection campaign. On the other hand, attorney Clark M. Clifford, former adviser to President Harry Truman and U.S. secretary of defense in the Lyndon Johnson administration, argues that a single six-year term is too long for an ineffective president and not enough time for an effective president to carry out his agenda. The resolution, known as S.J. Res. 77, was not passed, allowing Amendment XXII, which limits presidential tenure to two four-year terms, to stand firm in the Constitution.

Pro: Senator Mike Mansfield, Montana Democrat

I welcome the chance to express my views pertaining to the proposed Constitutional Amendment that would limit the Presidency to a single term of six years. I am particularly proud and pleased to join with the distinguished Senator from Vermont [George D. Aiken] in this endeavor which I personally regard as one of the most important reforms that our system of government could undergo.

Senate Committee on the Judiciary, testimony, Senate Constitutional Amendments Subcommittee, Washington, DC, October 28, 1971.

In recent years there have been a number of significant amendments to the Constitution of the United States. Correcting the matter of Presidential succession and particularly extending the franchise of the ballot to young adults 18, 19 and 20 years of age represent enormous steps forward: steps that protect and enhance immensely the Democratic processes of this Nation. In my judgment there is still another step that must be taken in this area of Constitutional evolution. It is only in providing a single Presidential term of six years, I believe, that this Nation will preserve for its highest office a sufficient degree of freedom and independence to function properly and adequately today and in the years ahead; years that will produce enormous trials and tensions on the national and global scale, some of which have yet to emerge.

By no means do I intend to imply that with this proposed amendment new ground is being broken or that a topic of first impression is here being raised. Indeed, the suggestion of a single six-year term has been with us ever since the delegates to the Constitutional Convention of 1787 thrashed over the question of a President's term and his eligibility for re-election. It is interesting to note that popular election was not considered with any great favor at all during the proceedings of that convention. But proposals limiting the tenure of the President were put forth and discussed. Ultimately none were approved and the question then became moot when the suggestion for an electoral college system gained the widest support.

Since the Constitution was ratified hundreds of amendments have been introduced in the Senate and House of Representatives proposing a change in Presidential tenure. More than 130 of these recommended a single term of six years. Twice, the House reported legislation providing for the six-year term. And in 1913, the Senate passed S.J. Res. 78 calling for a term of six years, but no action was taken by the other body. Presidents themselves have been most active in their support for the concept. Nearly 150 years ago Andrew Jackson recommended that the electoral college be abolished—also a good suggestion—that the President be elected by direct vote, and that he be limited to a single term of either four or six years. Presidents [Rutherford B.] Hayes and [Grover] Cleveland and William Howard Taft also offered the proposal. In more recent years on this issue I have followed the lead of the able and distinguished Senator from Vermont, the dean of the Republicans and a wise and prudent judge on all matters and particularly on those affecting the needs of democratic institutions in a rapidly changing world. That brings us up to today, and I must say that the merits of the proposal dictate its need now as never before.

It is just intolerable that a President of the United States—any President, whatever his party—is compelled to devote his time, energy and talents to what can be termed only as purely political tasks. I do not refer solely to a President's own re-election campaign. To be sure a re-election effort and all it entails are burdens enough. But a President facing re-election faces as well a host of demands that range from attending to the needs of political office holders, office seekers, financial backers and all the rest, to riding herd on the day-to-day developments within the pedestrian partisan arena. Surely this amendment does not represent a panacea for these ills which have grown up with our system of democracy. But it would go far, I think, in unsaddling the Presidency from many of these unnecessary political burdens that an incumbent bears.

Clearly such a change to a very great extent would free the President to devote a far greater measure of his time to the enormous task of serving all of the people of this Nation as Chief Executive. More time would thus be provided for policy-making and policy-implementing, for program initiating and for shaping and directing the kind of Administration a President chooses. More time would be provided for the kind of experimentation that a successful Presidency requires; such experimentation has come too infrequently in recent years, and as a Nation we suffer from that inadequacy.

In short, six full years could be devoted to the job of the Presidency, in and of itself, a complicated and gigantic responsibility. Six years could be devoted, free of the burdens of seeking—however unavoidably—partisan political objectives free of any potential conflicts inherent in such endeavors.

There is another aspect to this problem of re-election and it concerns not an incumbent President but rather those of the opposition: those who seek to gain the White House for their own. Certainly there is a great deal of room for constructive criticism, be it partisan or of whatever nature. Criticism is fundamental to our success as a Nation. It is what distinguishes us most as a free and open society. But there is another sort of criticism that a first term President must face at times and no President can give his fullest attention to the country so long as he is barraged and fired upon by those who do not offer constructive advice and alternatives but who would instead hope only to weaken an incumbent's chances for re-election. The effect of such vituperation when resorted to is just as invidious to the present two-term system as when an incumbent for similar partisan reasons puts political expediency before the Nation's interest. The President should be free to concentrate completely on his responsibilities. Electing him to a single term of six years, I think, would increase this probability.

And what of the arguments against this proposition? One raises the lame duck issue. The argument goes that when a President is elected for a single term of six years, he immediately becomes a lame duck. But the same is true today as soon as a President has been re-elected to a second term. The Twenty-second Amendment saw to that. But it is really no argument at all. Lameness by no means is inherent in a single term. It relates in my judgment to the strength and quality of the man holding the office; should he be a lame duck President it is not because of any inhibitions imposed by a single term. An unlimited number of terms would not sustain such a man. On the other hand, a President who rises to his responsibilities will have sufficient opportunity to organize an effective and successful Administration given a six-year term to do so. Six years in office is sufficient time to effectuate all such policy aims a newly-elected President entertains.

Conversely, six years is also long enough for one man to endure in a position filled with the pressures and tensions, the worries and responsibilities of the Presidency of the United States. Adding to them the stresses and strains of a re-election campaign simply makes no sense today. There are additional reasons. With a single six-year term, gone would be the charge, however invalid, that a President uses his power to appoint to achieve political ends and to pave the way for his re-election. For that matter, gone too would be the argument that discussions of foreign policy, of economics, and whatever, would be politically motivated.

Then there is the matter of election costs. The price of a Presidential campaign today has skyrocketed beyond reason. Should the trend continue, what is faced every four years in terms of financial burdens can only lead to the financial ruin of one or more of our national parties. Spreading that financial strain to six-year intervals should certainly ease some of the burden. Not to mention easing the burden that the electorate is compelled to undergo every four years. I think it would be welcome news in every household that the drawn out and tiresome events of national conventions and Presidential campaigns would at least occur with less frequency.

To sum it up, what this amendment seeks is to place the office of the Presidency in a position that transcends as much as possible partisan political considerations of whatever nature and source. That it cannot do the job completely, I would agree. The man who achieves the office carries with him his full political heritage. But its adoption would do much, I think, to streamline the Presidency in a manner that ultimately will make the position more fully responsive to the concerns of all Americans. . . .

Con: Clark M. Clifford, Attorney at Law

The concept of a single presidential term with reelection precluded has attracted adherents throughout our history. Many of the participants in the Constitutional Convention strongly advocated a single term. Between 1789 and 1947, when the Twenty-Second Amendment was approved by Congress, at least 270 resolutions were introduced in the Senate and the House to limit eligibility for reelection. Proponents of a fixed single term have included several of our Presidents. At one time or another, men of such diverse views as William Jennings Bryan, Horace Greeley, Everett Dirksen, Emanuel Celler and the present Majority Leader, Senator Mike Mansfield, have expressed support for a single term for Presidents. The notion was embraced in the Democratic Party Platform of 1912. It continues to enjoy substantial and distinguished support today—in the Senate, among newspaper columnists and among former White House aides. A former close adviser of President Franklin Roosevelt, Rexford Tugwell, has proposed that we elect our Presidents for a single nine-year term subject only to the ability of a President to secure a 40 per cent approval rating in a referendum at the end of his third year.

As I understand the support for restrictions on a President's right to stand for reelection, it derives from two basic motivations. The first is the continuing apprehension that a chief executive may find some means to perpetuate himself in power and thus assume the role of a dictator to the destruction of our liberties. This, it seems clear, was the motivating drive and political argument that led to the passage of the Twenty-Second Amendment in the aftermath of Franklin Roosevelt's election for four consecutive terms. I regard this as an unfounded fear in view of the constitutional distribution of powers and the certainty that a strong Congress and an informed electorate could and would protect themselves from any executive abuse.

The second argument is that a single presidential term without the possibility of reelection would free the President from political and partisan consideration and would enable him to devote his full energies to our vital concerns in the fields of national security, economic and social progress and improvements in the quality of life. The contention is that a single term would discourage such harassment and free the President from the millstone of partisan politics.

As I understand the selection of six years as the preferred term under Senate Joint Resolution 77, it is intended to balance the desirability of some continuity against the chance that a President might early in a longer term lose the popular support necessary to the development and implementation of his programs. Perhaps a subsidiary consideration is that the demands on our Presidents today are so complex and exhausting that no one should be required to accept election for a period greater than six years.

I disagree with the reasoning offered in support of Joint Resolution 77, and I would be strongly opposed to its adoption.

I agree with former President Woodrow Wilson's reasons for his opposition to single four or six-year terms: "Four years is too long a term for a President who is not the true spokesman of the people, who is imposed upon and does not lead. It is too short a term for a President who is doing, or attempting a great work of reform, and who has not had time to finish it. To change the term to six years would be to increase the likelihood of its being too long, without any assurance that it would, in happy cases, be long enough."

In essence, the ideal held out in Resolution 77 is a President with adequate time to see his major programs through and able to give his undivided attention to the national welfare without being diverted by political considerations, including those which derive from his quite human interest in re-election.

It is difficult to disagree with these objectives of ridding a President of both unfair political attack and undue political pressures. But on analysis, and based on the personal experience which it has been my privilege to obtain through association with several American Presidents, I find the notion that a President should be above politics inconsistent with our system of government, just as I find the prospect of a presidential dictator to be inconceivable under that same system.

Let me deal first with the argument that strict limits on the number of years a President may serve is necessary to protect against excessive presidential power. Viewed from that standpoint, the effect of Senate Joint Resolution 77 would be to cut the maximum presidential term from a tradition of eight years to one of six years. I recognize that under the Twenty-Second Amendment a maximum tenure of ten years would be possible if a President were to die in office and his Vice President were thereafter to be elected for two terms. But whether viewed as a two or a four-year constriction of the present limit on presidential service, I regard the proposed Amendment as completely unnecessary and thoroughly undesirable. I believe we denigrate ourselves as an enlightened people, and our political process as a whole, in imposing on ourselves still further disability to retain tested and trusted leadership. The Congress and the judiciary are now, and will remain, free to utilize their own countervailing constitutional power to forestall any executive overreaching. And I see no reason to apprehend that a President will act less wisely, or less discreetly, in his seventh or ninth year in office than he does in his first six years.

Alexander Hamilton appropriately noted: "How unwise must be every such self-denying ordinance as serves to prohibit a nation from making use of its own citizens, in the manner best suited to its exigencies and circumstances." Surely we should not amend our Constitution to deny ourselves the opportunity to elect the best man in a time of great need.

I turn now to the contention that a single six-year term would free the President from the pressures of party politics. I must say that I regard this as neither practical nor desirable. Under our two-party system, which I believe well serves the interests of a country as large and as heterogeneous as our own, most Presidents will have risen to prominence through the partisan political process. With rare exceptions, they will previously have held elective office. They will, and I believe it is a healthy fact, owe some continued allegiance to the party which propelled them to the highest office our Nation can award.

But as long as we have political parties, no President can hope to be free from political attack, whether or not he is free to run for reelection. The party out of power will continue to be critical, to be partisan and even at times to be unfair. The opposition party objective is not just to remove an individual but to substitute a President of its own political persuasion. I regard it as unrealistic to expect that a party which has lost the presidency will be significantly more indulgent to the victor because he cannot be a candidate again.

Instead, I would expect that the restriction of a President to a single term would lessen his political support rather than the amount of political attack. A President, to be effective, needs all the support he can get. He requires the confidence and the sympathy of the American public. He requires the co-operation of Congressmen and Senators on both sides of the aisle. But he certainly can hope to accomplish little unless he has the active and willing support of most members of his own party.

Our political parties are not subject to the rigid discipline that exists in some countries, particularly those with a parliamentary form of government. But the Senators and Congressmen politically aligned with the President are the most responsive means by which he can enact and implement his programs.

Without help and support from his party, presidential power becomes very limited and formal, demonstrable for the most part in negative ways—by vetoes, resistance to reform and opposition to the new ideas of others. Only the politically talented leader, sensitive to the political currents of the day and in close alliance with political leaders in and out of Washington, can forge the necessary coalitions that can get things done.

The Twenty-Second Amendment seriously erodes a President's power during his second term. The substitution of an even tighter limit on presidential tenure such as Resolution 77 would handicap him from his first day in office. He, of course, would retain the full legal powers vested in him by the Constitution and laws of the United States. But he has lost a significant degree of political power and, in a governmental system characterized by two powerful political parties, this is an important ingredient in presidential effectiveness.

A President who can never again be a candidate is a President whose coattails are permanently in mothballs. Those of his party in the Congress and in the States will of course retain an interest in the building of a good record of party accomplishments, but his personal bargaining position is nonetheless seriously weakened. The other strong political figures in his party may continue to look to him as their leader—but many will also see him primarily as their predecessor.

The political disadvantage of a fixed and unrenewable term will also show its effects within the Executive Branch itself. A President's ability to make his mark on our vast and sprawling government derives primarily from his power to appoint. Through those whom he places in Cabinet and sub-Cabinet positions, he tries to see that the institutional inertia of all large organizations will not frustrate his programs and objectives. But in the waning years of a fixed and final term, it will become harder for a President to attract people of the caliber and competence he needs to help him operate a government of this size and complexity. The men and women best equipped for high political appointment are necessarily individuals already engaged in important and useful work. They are asked to disrupt their personal and professional lives, usually at significant financial sacrifice. They must compare these costs with the rewards of participation in matters of great public importance. When they recognize that the President whom they are asked to serve must himself be out of office within a year or two, they can hardly be blamed if they conclude that the price for so brief a period of government service is disproportionately high.

Many of these difficulties obviously are inherent in the present situation under the Twenty-Second Amendment. I believe that they would, however, be greatly increased by the substitution of a single six-year term in which the terminal date of a President's service is known from the time he is first elected.

Most of our Presidents have been politicians. Those who were not, and who were successful, became politicians. Politics does not always enjoy a good name. But politics, in the final analysis, is an essential part of democracy. A President above politics is a President remote from the processes of government and removed from the thoughts and aspirations of his people.

The objective of constitutional reform should be to attract the best leadership and improve the ability of such leaders to perform at their greatest effectiveness. It is my firm conviction that the imposition of a rigid restriction on presidential tenure is inconsistent with that objective.

Amendment XXII Limits Presidential Effectiveness

David A. Crockett

In the following viewpoint, David A. Crockett explores the idea that Amendment XXII creates ineffective "lame duck" presidents who have limited presidential power at the end of their second terms. Crockett examines the arguments for and against presidential term limits, citing the opinions of Alexander Hamilton and Thomas Jefferson, who differed on the subject of limiting the time a person can serve as president. Hamilton believed that a president should serve as many terms as the people wanted, creating stability in the executive branch and bringing a certain amount of accountability to the office of the presidency. Jefferson, on the other hand, argued that term limits on the presidency were necessary to prevent a tyranny and a monarchial form of government. Crockett believes that Hamilton's arguments are more solid than Jefferson's and that term limits do more harm than good, forcing a rotation of office and creating ineffective second-term presidents who accomplish little in their final years in office.

Crockett is an associate professor of political science at Trinity University in San Antonio, Texas.

Well into President George W. Bush's second term, history appears to be repeating itself—second terms are far more problematic than first terms. Are problematic second terms inevitable, and if so are they caused by the Twenty-second Amendment?

David A. Crockett, "The Contemporary Presidency: 'An Excess of Refinement': Lame Duck Presidents in Constitutional and Historical Context," *Presidential Studies Quarterly*, vol. 38, December 2008, p. 707. Copyright © 2008 by Center for the Study of the Presidency. Reproduced by permission of Sage Publications, Inc.

Lame Duck Status

As this article is being written [December 2008], the nation is well into the final quartile of President George W. Bush's presidency, and it would appear that history is repeating itself. Despite a reelection win that was clearly stronger than his first victory, and despite claiming political capital he was willing to spend, Bush's second term has witnessed plunging public approval, a troubled policy agenda, and significant midterm election losses. The administration entered its second term having undertaken a study of previous second terms to stave off the inevitable, to no apparent avail. History demonstrates that second terms are far more problematic than first terms, afflicted with "sixth year itches," "sixth year curses," and the more generic "second term blues."

One explanation for this phenomenon is the president's status as a lame duck due to the term limits imposed by the Twenty-second Amendment . . . concluding that term limits are, in [Alexander] Hamilton's evocative phrase, "an excess of refinement."

The question of term limits and presidential effectiveness in second terms is important not because of the president's desire to be successful by winning specific policy battles or getting his way, but because the various functions . . . are important for the effectiveness of republican government in general. The qualities provided by energetic leadership and clerkship—the broader goals of security and stability—ideally would not be contingent upon election cycles and duration in office. That is, perhaps, too ideal a vision, but the framers of the Constitution wrestled with these questions at the constitutional convention, recognizing the connection between the selection process, tenure of office, and the ability of the president to fulfill these functions. Multiple terms would make a president selected by Congress too dependent on that body, defeating the theory behind separation of powers and doing great harm to the function of leadership. If being eligible for

Protesters dressed as Mussolini and Roman guards speak out against Mayor Michael Bloomberg and the October 2008 vote to extend term limits by the New York City Council. Image copyright ParryPix, 2009. Used under license from Shutterstock.com.

reelection, for whatever reason, is desirable, selection would have to be done by some other mechanism. While the original debate was over whether the president should be limited to one term only, the existence of any term limit has the potential to impact these important and essential functions. It is to the question of term limits that we now turn.

The Core Debate

Although the Twenty-second Amendment to the Constitution was ratified in a largely partisan effort with surprisingly little substantive deliberation in Congress, the argument for term limits has a solid and respectable pedigree. Contrary to popular belief, however, that pedigree does not begin with George Washington. The first president did not intentionally establish the so-called two-term tradition; his departure was motivated by a desire to demonstrate that the country could function without him and to retire to Mount Vernon. He made no principled argument for limiting presidents to two terms, and in fact disagreed with Thomas Jefferson on this point. While Jefferson made use of Washington's voluntary retirement, calling it "the sound precedent set by an illustrious predecessor," it was Jefferson himself who gave philosophical justification to the two-term limit. In his 1807 letter to the Vermont Legislature, Jefferson outlined two major concerns behind his belief in some sort of fixed limit of terms. First, Jefferson articulates the common American fear of excessive executive power, arguing that unlimited reeligibility would cause the presidency to become monarchical and degenerate "into an inheritance." Second, Jefferson mentions his concern for the effect of age on the body and the mind, fearing the "decline which advancing years bring on." To summarize, Jefferson's twin concerns are with the potential for tyranny and the health and vitality of the chief executive. The concern about tyranny can be interpreted as a fear that the leadership function of the presidency would be corrupted in monarchical directions. The concern about health relates to the weakness any institution would experience when it is composed of one person who is not operating at full strength and capacity.

Jefferson's heirs followed his lead, particularly James Madison, James Monroe, and Andrew Jackson, but it can hardly be said that a two-term tradition was clearly settled in the 19th century. In fact, the philosophy of the Whig Party was even stricter, calling for a one-term limit, something the two elected Whig generals complied with by dying in office. Other presidents from both major parties pledged at various times to serve only one term, including James K. Polk and Rutherford B. Hayes. There were also presidents from both parties—Ulysses Grant, Theodore Roosevelt, and Woodrow Wilson—who attempted to gain the nomination for a third term, though all failed. In spite of these exceptions, however, the two-term tradition was established enough to prompt significant comment when Franklin D. Roosevelt chose to run for a third term in 1940.

By contrast, the argument for unlimited reeligibility was made most powerfully by Alexander Hamilton, writing as Publius in Federalist No. 72. Where Jefferson is most concerned with tyranny and health, Hamilton is focused primarily on the desire for stability in the administration of government. He sees term limits as a device that would require change both in leadership and the administration of the laws. All presidents have an incentive, in Hamilton's view, to reverse the policies and change the personnel of their predecessors. Their need to establish their own legacies and reputations results in "a disgraceful and ruinous mutability in the administration of the government." At the same time, the impossibility of reelection would reduce the incentives for presidents to pursue worthy projects, since they would not be able to take credit for them. This second argument links the discussion of term limits to the larger one of accountability in the executive branch. . . .

Accountability Best Without Limits

Having laid out these core arguments, it is a simple matter to evaluate them in light of the central functions of the executive branch established by the framers. What little deliberation took place about the Twenty-second Amendment centered on the first of Jefferson's concerns. Republicans and conservative Democrats, agitated by the "dictatorship" set up by Franklin D. Roosevelt and Harry Truman, made reference to Jefferson's precedent and the fear of executive tyranny. It is difficult to take Jefferson's argument seriously, however, in light of the constitutional structure. The foundation for his argument against tyranny is his belief that "a representative government, responsible at short periods of election, is that which produces the greatest sum of happiness to mankind." The framers of the Constitution may have agreed with him, but they chose to focus the greatest amount of accountability in the House of Representatives. Publius recognizes that republican government in general needs to have "an immediate dependence on, and an intimate sympathy with, the people," and that link can only be accomplished by "frequent elections." That is why members of the House serve for only two years—it is the most democratic and responsive of the federal institutions. . . .

Similarly, four-year terms for the president allow the chief executive to protect "the interests of the people" when their inclinations endanger them. A strong concern for security and liberty lies at the heart of the structure of tenure, with the goal of simple democracy secondary in the branches that have lengthier terms of office. Jefferson's argument ignores the fact that the presidency is not designed to be a purely representative institution, and forced rotation in office is not a top concern for a branch focused on security and stability. Conversely, while the unitary nature of the presidency allows for greater accountability to the people as the chief executive performs his function, term limits reduce that sense of accountability as the president realizes he no longer has to face the proverbial music. This incentive is not completely eliminated, for presidents desire to establish a legacy and reputation, and one way of doing that is to ensure the election of a successor from their party. However, the very attempt to secure a legacy can run counter to the interests of the heir apparent, who may have his own vision of what the incumbent should be doing to help secure his election. . . .

Hamilton's Arguments

Term limits, in Hamilton's view, work against all the major objectives of the presidency. First, they require a change in agenda-setting where one may not be necessary. Hamilton fears that term limits will prompt presidents to ignore worthy projects, since the president will not be able to take credit for them. Whether that fear is true, the conventional wisdom is that term limits prevent presidents from pursuing bold projects, even if they want to. Indeed, perhaps the most common criticism of the two-term limit is that it makes the president an instant lame duck, thus reducing the power and influence of the president as a policy leader. Because they cannot run for office again, presidents have a diminished ability to shape the policy agenda. We know with certainty that George W. Bush will no longer be president at noon, January 20, 2009. There is no mystery about that fact. As that time approaches, political actors both at the national and international level may opt to wait for the next administration for action. While this type of reasoning could take place during any contested election, the absolute certainly or departure that comes with term limits encourages such gamesmanship far more than a first term contest where reelection is a real possibility.

This seems especially true after the sixth year, when the political class begins to look forward to the next presidential election—a process that begins earlier and lasts longer with each passing election cycle. The election drama occupies more and more news media space, and the result is that the president has little power to start new projects, whether social security reform, immigration reform, or comprehensive health care reform. Perversely enough, a president is most powerful in agenda-setting as he starts his first term, when he is least experienced and knowledgeable. When his knowledge and experience are at their highest, starting a second term, his political capital—contra George W. Bush—only gets lower. The president does not lack incentives to pursue bold projects—his desire to establish a legacy and reputation overrides the dampening effect of term limits—but the structure of the system works against that desire. Accounts of Roosevelt's decision to run for a third term—something he did not declare definitively until the 1940 Democratic National Convention—demonstrate his ability to retain political influence through most of his second term simply because of doubts about the succession.

Of course, the veto remains a powerful agenda-influencing tool, even if it is a negative one, throughout a president's administration, and recent research demonstrates that a president's ability to pursue unilateral policy-making through executive orders gives presidents additional leadership tools. Successful efforts to secure balanced budgets by [Dwight] Eisenhower and [Bill] Clinton and the 1986 tax reform act signed by [Ronald] Reagan demonstrate that significant things can be accomplished after first terms have ended. Nevertheless, term limits mark a weakening of this aspect of leadership, one that often appears to begin the day following reelection.

Changes May Threaten Security

Second, Hamilton believes term limits could require a change in leadership during a national emergency, thus threatening the security of the nation. This is precisely the argument Roosevelt used to justify running for a third term. Of course, the nation has changed hands before in the middle of a war, and the experience of George W. Bush after the terrorist strikes on 9/11—his rapid rise in popular approval—demonstrates the tremendous power even a constrained president can wield when performing his leadership function in the service of national security. In fact, the constraints term limits presumably place on a president's agenda-setting abilities in the domestic arena may prompt him to take more vigorous action in the foreign policy realm, where his power to lead is naturally less constrained.

A short list of significant activities proving that energy does not have to dissipate with term limits would include Eisenhower's second-term efforts to "wage peace," Reagan's Berlin Wall speech and successful intermediate nuclear force (INF) treaty with the Soviet Union, and Clinton's military action in Kosovo and Middle East peace efforts. The issue for Hamilton has less to do with the ability of presidents to act in times of crisis than with forcing change in the middle of a crisis, whether the country desires that change or not. Roosevelt's own experience testifies to the ambiguity Americans feel about this question, for his reelections to third and fourth terms came by smaller and smaller margins, but he was, nevertheless, strongly elected all four times, demonstrating the public's relative satisfaction with his leadership. Presidents may suffer the conceit of thinking they are indispensable, as Roosevelt reportedly did prior to 1940, but that vice may prove a relatively minor one if the benefit is continued leadership by an experienced hand. Of course, popular disapproval of crisis management will lead to a change in leadership. . . .

Term Limits Add Nothing Positive

One common suggestion to reform the presidency has been to move toward a system of six-year terms with no reeligibility. Had that system been put in place from the beginning, the nation would have seen an average of 3.33 presidents every 20 years—very close to the historical reality. Given Hamilton's original proposal that the president serve for life it is doubtful that this rate of change would be satisfactory to him, but it is clear that the institution of term limits has had little effect on rotation in office. Of course, whether or not the presidency itself changes hands, it is common for any administration to witness significant change in cabinet and advisory positions. Term limits, with the sure knowledge of impending change at the top, may prompt a larger number of resignations as bureaucratic leaders seek employment elsewhere. Hamilton would question why there is a requirement for change when, for all the reasons stipulated above, it is unnecessary.

From a constitutional perspective, then, it would appear that term limits provide little to the political system. They introduce the element of forced rotation where the original design of the office was biased in favor of stability and longevity, assuming competent performance, especially in the areas of administration and crisis management. They work to hamper the president's agenda-setting function in the second term, though presidents can compensate for that fact somewhat through the use of other executive tools. They do not act as much of a constraint in the foreign policy arena, where the president's natural structural advantages favor independent action. They allow a president to pay less attention to "the restraints of public opinion," since they know they have won their last victory, though presidents remain interested in helping their partisan heirs ratify their reputation with a victory. Other than a mandated rotation in office, then, the only thing term limits provide is a hedge against the political leader whose ambition may prompt him to serve beyond his physical and mental abilities.

Amendment XXII Does Not Limit Presidential Power

William G. Howell and Kenneth R. Mayer

In the following viewpoint, authors William G. Howell and Kenneth R. Mayer argue that Amendment XXII does not limit the power of the president and that, in most cases, the commander in chief remains an effective leader until his final days in office. The authors point out that many presidents, even though they are considered "lame ducks" since their successors will soon take over the Oval Office, still wield enough political power to enact effective policy changes. From John Adams to Bill Clinton, presidents have used their last days in office to effectuate lasting policy changes, both foreign and domestic, often without the support of Congress. Howell is the Sydney Stein Professor in American Politics at the Harris School of Public Policy Studies at the University of Chicago, and Mayer is a professor of political science at the University of Wisconsin–Madison. Both have authored books on U.S. presidential power.

A curious thing happens during the last one hundred days of a presidential administration: political uncertainty shifts to political certitude. The president knows exactly who will succeed him—his policy positions, his legislative priorities, and the level of partisan support he will enjoy within the new Congress. And if the sitting president (or his party) lost the election, he has every reason to hurry through last-minute public policies, doing whatever possible to tie his successor's hands.

Can he succeed? . . . Defeated at the polls in November and guaranteed political retirement in January, an outgoing

William G. Howell and Kenneth R. Mayer, "The Last One Hundred Days (of Presidential Campaigns)," *Presidential Studies Quarterly*, vol. 35, September 2005, pp. 533–53. Copyright © 2005 by Presidential Studies Quarterly. Reproduced by permission of Sage Publications, Inc.

president has little ground upon which to advocate for his (someday her) policy agenda. During his final months in office, his public prestige and professional reputation—the ingredients of persuasion, and the purported foundations of presidential power—run empty. Members of Congress have little cause to do a defeated president's bidding; and without them, presidents cannot hope to accomplish anything of consequence. As such, outgoing presidents have little choice but to recognize their plight, gather their belongings, and close the door on their administration.

History Proves Pessimists Wrong

In our estimation, this misconstrues things. By ignoring important policy options outside of the legislative process, scholars have exaggerated the frailty of outgoing presidents and underestimated the influence they continue to wield. Presidential power does not reduce to bargaining, negotiating, and convincing members of Congress to do things that the president cannot accomplish on his own. Presidents can (and regularly do) act alone, setting public policy without having to rally Congress's attention, nor even its support. With executive orders, proclamations, executive agreements, national security directives, and memoranda, presidents have ample resources to effectuate policy changes that stand little chance of overcoming the collective action problems and multiple veto points that plague the legislative process. And having "lost the attention of the permanent government," outgoing presidents have every reason to strike out on their own, set new policy, and leave it to the incoming administration to try and steer an alternative course.

Examples of last-minute presidential actions abound. It was President John Adams's "Midnight" appointments, which Jefferson refused to honor, that prompted the landmark *Marbury v. Madison* Supreme Court decision. Grover Cleveland created a twenty-one-million-acre forest reserve to prevent logging, an act that led to an unsuccessful impeachment attempt and the passage of legislation annulling the action. Then, in response to the congressional uprising [as Nancy Combs stated,] "Cleveland issued a pocket veto and left office." Jimmy Carter negotiated for the release of Americans held hostage in Tehran, implementing an agreement on his last day in office with ten separate executive orders, many of which sharply restricted the rights of private parties to sue the Iranian government for expropriation of their property. It was, according to Harold Hongju Koh, "One of the most dramatic exercises of presidential power in foreign affairs in peacetime United States history." In late December 1992, George [H.W.] Bush pardoned six [Ronald] Reagan administration officials who were involved in the Iran-Contra scandal, a step that ended Independent Counsel Lawrence Walsh's criminal investigation. "[In] a single stroke, Mr. Bush swept away one conviction, three guilty pleas, and two pending cases, virtually decapitating what was left of Mr. Walsh's effort, which began in 1986." During his final days in office [Bill] Clinton "issued scads of executive orders" on issues ranging from protecting the Hawaiian Islands Coral Reef Ecosystem Reserve to prohibiting the importation of rough cut diamonds from Sierra Leone to curbing tobacco use both domestically and abroad. . . .

Presidential Transitions

There is, at present, a sizable literature on presidential transitions. Without exception, this work places incoming presidents (aides and advisers brought in tow) front and center. The literature really is about the challenges of moving from a campaign to a governing stance, of transforming former governors, senators, and vice presidents into presidents, of preparing November victors for the awesome responsibilities and powers that await them in January. It spells out the issues of staffing, management, agenda setting, and policy formulation that inevitably confront presidents-elect. It catalogs the personal and professional tensions—between policy and political advisers, between campaign workers and governing staffers, between Washington insiders and loyal aides from the president-elect's home state—that regularly infect transitions. Much of this literature, further, has a strong prescriptive element. It offers up advice to newly elected presidents—delineate clearly lines of authority; delegate wisely; heed the importance of management; promote loyalty, though not at the expense of free and open dialogue—in the hopes that they will avoid the mistakes of past transitions. This literature, in short, details how former presidential candidates steady their sights on the presidency itself, lay the groundwork for governance, and, if they are lucky, generate the momentum needed for change. . . .

Writes [historian] Carl Brauer, during presidential transitions "formal authority continues to reside in the occupant of the White House, [but] his political power is small compared to that of his successor. The focus of attention is on the person about to become President, not on the person about to vacate the office." Laurin Henry [an expert on presidential transitions] characterizes outgoing presidents as "caretakers" who enjoy three final months to close up shop and ease into retirement. The sitting president's policy agenda, his independent interests and initiatives, along with the powers he wielded during the prior three and three-quarter years, quickly dissipate in the waning months of his administration, as attention rightfully shifts to the newly elected president and the spectacle of a new government being formed. . . .

Setting Policy Unilaterally

Portraits of outgoing presidents going quietly into the night overlook an important feature of American politics, and of executive power—namely, the president's ability to unilaterally set public policy. Using executive orders, proclamations, executive agreements, national security directives, memoranda, and other directives, presidents have at their disposal a wide variety of means to effectuate lasting and substantive policy changes, both foreign and domestic. Because they do not depend upon the active support or cooperation of Congress, these tools of direct action present ample opportunities for presidential influence, influence that has very little to do with bargaining or persuasion. "With the stroke of the pen," these actions assume the weight of law. And so they remain until and unless someone else overturns them.

A basic principle governs the production of unilateral directives: presidential policy making rises as Congress's capacity to legislate declines. If Congress cannot get its act together— either because of partisan divisions within its membership or the timing of the electoral calendar—presidents have strong incentives to exercise their unilateral powers. For indeed, when gridlock prevails within Congress, presidents can (and regularly do) strike out on their own and set policies that would not survive the legislative process. . . .

Incentives to exercise these unilateral powers, as such, should intensify in the final stages of a presidential administration. It is then that Congress is least likely to do the president's bidding because, all agree, his powers to bargain, negotiate, and persuade have diminished. It is also then that the legislative process grinds to a virtual standstill, assuring that little effort will be expended on advancing his agenda— nor, by extension, on reversing policy directives that the president issues on his own. Precisely because legislative success rates taper off at the end of a term, unilateral activity should spike upward.

Not all transitions, however, invite unilateral activity. When the office passes from Republican to Republican, or Democrat to Democrat, the sitting president has little cause to hurry through a slew of last-minute directives. A reelected incumbent need not issue a slate of unilateral directives during the final months of his first term; nor does an outgoing president who is to be replaced by a co-partisan. Emerging victorious in November, these presidents are assured of four more years in service of their legislative agendas. Rather, it is when the incumbent's party loses that presidents should exercise these powers with exceptional zeal, making final impressions on public policy in the short time before the opposition party assumes control.

Patterns of Unilateral Activity

Our empirical expectations are straightforward: presidential transitions should witness jumps in unilateral activity when power switches from one party to the other; but transitions from first to second terms, and transitions from co-partisans, should not impact the frequency with which presidents issue unilateral policy directives.

Some preliminary evidence already supports our expectations. Kenneth Mayer has demonstrated that presidents issue nearly twice as many executive orders (exempting purely administrative orders) during the final month of those terms when they are leaving office to a successor of the opposite party. Mayer finds no effects during transitions between first- and second-term presidents, or in the final month that divides two presidents from the same party. In every one of Mayer's regressions, the observed impact of presidential transitions on unilateral activity is substantially larger than those observed for all other explanatory variables. The results, further, hold irrespective of whether one examines the 1939–99 or the 1949–99 time period. These findings, according to Mayer, give credence to the contention "that executive orders have a strong policy component, as otherwise presidents would have little reason to issue such last-minute orders." . . .

Based on the random sample of orders issued between 1945 and 1999, presidents issued, on average, 1.08 significant orders during each of the last three months of their terms.

During transitions from first to second terms, and from incumbents to newly elected presidents from the same party, 1.32 significant orders are issued. But when presidents, or their parties, lose the office to the opposition, they issue an average of 2.34 significant orders during each of the final three months of office—almost twice the average level of activity recorded during the modern era. . . .

Making Orders Stick

How long do last-minute presidential actions endure? Surely, what an outgoing president accomplishes unilaterally in the twilight of his administration, the incoming president can undo unilaterally during his honeymoon. Presidents regularly issue executive orders, proclamations, and rules that overturn unilateral actions taken by their predecessors. And should they prefer not to overturn an order, newly elected presidents can simply block its implementation. Just as Reagan imposed a sixty-day moratorium on the implementation of rules that Carter instituted during the last three months of his administration, so did [George W.] Bush, immediately upon taking office, put a halt to orders that Clinton issued in the waning days of his administration.

It would be a mistake, however, to conclude that the bursts of unilateral activity that occur in the final months of an outgoing president's administration ultimately, indeed almost immediately, amount to little more than last gasps of a discredited regime. Occasionally, presidents cannot alter orders set by their predecessors without paying a considerable political price, undermining the nation's credibility, or confronting serious legal obstacles. Consider the following.

Outgoing presidents can impose a wide range of obligations on incoming presidents. Some of these commitments may come directly from the president, in the form of executive orders, proclamations, administrative directives, appointments, or other unilateral actions. Others may originate in executive branch agencies through the rulemaking process. And there are special advantages associated with pursuing this latter route. "[Once] a final regulation has been published in the Federal Register, the only unilateral way an administration can revise it is through new rulemaking under the Administrative Procedure Act. Agencies cannot change existing regulations arbitrarily; instead, they must first develop a factual record that supports the change in policy." If a lame-duck administration can hustle a final rule out the door before January 20th, the new administration must begin an entirely new cycle of rulemaking. Not only does this require time, but changing the status quo may well mean taking on interest groups who are reticent to give up ground that they have just won. . . .

Clinton's Final Proclamations

Clinton's high end-of-term energy had some consequences that Bush could not undo, even if he were so inclined. Throughout his terms, Clinton had aggressively used his delegated power under the 1906 Antiquities Act to establish numerous national monuments. Unlike many unilateral acts, though, these national monuments, once established by proclamation, could not be "disestablished" by a subsequent proclamation. The Antiquities Act, which Clinton used to legally justify his actions, only permits presidents to extend federal protections to new sires; nothing in the act allows presidents to weaken, much less retract, existing protections. The only way Bush could reverse Clinton's actions was to assemble the necessary majorities and supermajorities required to enact a law—a difficult feat indeed, given the multiple veto points and collective action problems that plague the legislative process.

Knowing this, Clinton issued a batch of proclamations during the final months of his administration that extended federal protections to more than 2 million acres of public lands. On November 9, 2001, Clinton issued proclamations 7373 and 7374 which expanded the protected lands in Craters of the Moon, Idaho and Vermilion Cliffs, Arizona. Then, just days before leaving office, Clinton issued proclamations 7392–99 and 7402, which created national monuments in the Virgin Islands, California, New Mexico, Idaho, Montana, Arizona, and New York totaling more than 1 million acres. And with executive orders 13178 and 13196 issued in December 2000 and January 2001, Clinton extended federal protections to fully 84 million acres of Hawaiian undersea coral reefs.

However much Bush might have objected to both the substance of Clinton's orders and the process by which they were issued, he lacked statutory authority to undo them unilaterally. Moreover, the Bush administration noted that any organized effort to overturn them legislatively would be pointless. In February 2001, Secretary of the Interior Gale Norton stated that while she "disapprove[d] of the process by which those monuments were generally created," there would be no effort to revoke them. In June 2001, Representative Mike Simpson (R-ID) introduced legislation to curb the president's authority under the Antiquities Act. Under the proposal, a president would have a difficult time creating national monuments larger than 50,000 acres. In these cases, the law imposes notification, consultation, and public comment. Crucially, it requires positive congressional action within two years to approve the designation. Although the bill was reported by the House Committee on Resources, no floor action occurred. Simpson reintroduced the bill in 2003 as H.R. 2386; as of this writing, the bill has yet to emerge from committee.

International Commitments

Last-minute domestic policy initiatives can . . . put the new administration in an uncomfortable (if not altogether untenable) position. There are times, however, when an outgoing president can create international commitments, which have the effect of putting the international prestige of the United States on the line. To be sure, a newly elected president can withdraw from international agreements negotiated by his predecessor—doing so, however, may damage relations with the other nations that were party to the agreement, just as they harm the United States' perceived credibility in the globe more generally. Consider two such examples, one involving a president's efforts to dissolve an international crisis, the other an effort to construct a new international court.

In 1981, outgoing President Carter used executive orders, many signed on his last day in office, to secure the release of American hostages held in the Tehran embassy since November 1979. These orders committed the United States to abide by a series of international agreements governing the disposition of claims against the Iranian government. Although it was within the Reagan administration's power to revoke them, the fact that Carter had used the orders to bind the nation to international law made the legal situation much more complicated than it would have otherwise been. . . . Although the Reagan administration was hardly enthusiastic about the agreement Carter had negotiated, officials ultimately saw no alternative to implementing it.

On December 31, 2000, Clinton announced that the United States would become a signatory to the Treaty of Rome, which established the International Criminal Court (ICC). The United States was one of seven nations to vote against the final treaty in 1998, largely because of concerns that the ICC would be able to assert jurisdiction over U.S. military personnel. "The principal objection raised by the administration . . . was that American nationals, particularly members of the armed services, could in certain contingencies be subjected to trial in the new court without the specific consent of the United States." But on the last day on which nations could sign, Clinton reversed course. And he did so without any intention of even submitting the treaty for Senate ratification. . . .

Clinton's decision did not formally bind the incoming administration to the ICC. Still, many international legal scholars argued that as a signatory, the United States did have an obligation under international law to refrain from actively working to undermine the treaty. But the Bush administration, along with Congress, remained strongly opposed to the ICC. . . .

In May 2002, shortly before the new ICC was set to enter into force, the White House announced its intention to "unsign" the treaty and renounce all obligations as a signatory, an act that UN officials claimed was unprecedented. . . .

The withdrawal did not attract a significant amount of public attention. But the move did (and continues to) complicate foreign policy, requiring the Bush administration to expend political capital that it might otherwise have been able to devote to other purposes. . . .

Contrary to conventional wisdom on the matter, presidents do not quietly relinquish their powers the moment that the nation votes them out of office. Instead, these presidents squeeze these last moments in office for all they are worth, issuing all sorts of rules and directives, many of which cannot be changed without exacting a significant political price to either the incoming president or to the nation as a whole. While legislative processes may lay dormant at the end of a presidential term, the production of unilateral directives kicks into high gear.

More generally, though, our analysis makes use of an emerging theoretical emphasis on the president's unilateral powers. We argue that presidents have always had a motive to wield their power up to the very last minute. Our contribution is a confirmation that presidents have the means to do so in ways that establish concrete and enduring policies—policies that the current Congress would likely refuse to enact, and that the succeeding president is sometimes forced to accept.

Reflecting upon the legitimacy of these "lame-duck" policies, we can distinguish between two types of last-minute presidential actions. The first are those that are consistent with the presidential preferences as expressed throughout his term, or which are merely an extension or continuation of existing policy. Because policy processes, even for unilateral actions, take time, a decision issued a week before the inauguration might reflect work that has been going on for months— even well before the election. The second category consists of those decisions that would not have been made had the president (or at least the president's party) been reelected. Such policies are either inconsistent with previous actions or are sufficiently controversial that they would have created unacceptable political consequences for the president. As we have noted, defeated presidents are no longer encumbered by the threat of electoral retribution; by definition, that threat has already been carried out. Outgoing presidents need no longer concern themselves about the electoral consequences of what they do during the transition, or about how a controversial decision will affect the rest of their agendas. A poorly considered act could, of course, affect a president's legacy, but that is more of a personal than a public concern.

Former Presidents Who Later Serve as Vice Presidents Would Not Violate Amendment XXII

Michael C. Dorf

In the following viewpoint, Michael C. Dorf explores the idea of a former president who has served two four-year terms serving as vice president under a new commander in chief. In 2000, when Dorf wrote this article, many speculated that Democratic presidential candidate Al Gore would choose former president Bill Clinton as his vice presidential running mate. This brought up the issue of the constitutionality of a president who has served eight years in office serving as vice president. As Dorf points out, the Constitution permits Clinton to be elected vice president and to act as president for a third time, if necessary. In the Clinton-Gore case, as Dorf argues, neither Amendment XXII nor Amendment XII—which states that any person who is constitutionally ineligible to the office of president is also ineligible to the office of vice president—can prevent former president Clinton from running as a vice presidential hopeful. Dorf is Robert S. Stevens Professor of Law at Cornell University Law School in Ithaca, New York.

Leading in most polls, Texas Governor George W. Bush [in the presidential election of 2000] had the luxury of allowing political calculations to take a back seat in his choice of a running mate. Rather than having to select a flashy personality from a large "battleground" state that might go either way in the election, Bush could afford to choose Wyoming's bland but experienced Dick Cheney as his veep hopeful.

Vice President Al Gore [Democratic presidential candidate in 2000], whose campaign needs a serious jumpstart, cannot afford a similar luxury. Instead, Gore must choose a running mate who would generate a sense of excitement. Who would be a better choice than the most charismatic and skillful politician of his generation—William Jefferson Clinton?

Indeed, *New York Times* editorialist Thomas L. Friedman has already suggested President Clinton as a potential veep choice for Gore. To be sure, Mr. Friedman made this suggestion jokingly—but Clinton's charisma is no joke. With Clinton on the ticket, many swing voters might choose Gore over Bush (although those suffering Clinton fatigue might well swing the other way).

Prognostication aside, the prospect of a Gore-Clinton ticket raises an interesting constitutional question: Can a man who has been President for eight years be elected and serve as Vice President?

The Constitutional Argument

Tremulous Republicans and other naysayers will no doubt claim that the Twenty-Second Amendment would bar a Clinton Vice-Presidency. This amendment—enacted after F.D.R. [Franklin Delano Roosevelt] was elected President for the fourth time—imposes a two-term limit on presidential candidates.

Now, the language of the amendment certainly does not *expressly* apply to a vice-presidential candidate. But other constitutional provisions guarantee that the Vice President becomes President upon the death, incapacity, impeachment, or resignation of the President. Thus, if a two-term President like Bill Clinton became Vice President, that would raise the specter of a possible third Clinton Presidential term—a specter which would become a reality if any of these unfortunate events were to befall a President Gore. Some might argue that, as a result, a Clinton Vice-Presidency (and that of any two-term President) would be unconstitutional.

President Bill Clinton and Vice President Al Gore in the Library of Congress, 1996. AP Images.

In support of this argument, one might also cite the Twelfth Amendment—which provides, in pertinent part, that "no person constitutionally ineligible to the office of President shall be eligible to that of Vice-President of the United States." President Clinton is certainly ineligible to be elected to another presidential term, based on the Twenty-Second Amendment. Some might infer from the Twelfth Amendment that he is therefore also ineligible to be elected to a vice-presidential term.

Entirely Constitutional

But these naysayers would be wrong. The Constitution permits Clinton to be elected Vice President, and if necessary to ascend for a third time to the Presidency—as careful attention to the language of the Twelfth and Twenty-Second Amendments shows.

The Twelfth Amendment would allow a Clinton Vice-Presidency. Its language only bars from the vice-presidency those persons who are "ineligible to the office" of President. Clinton is not ineligible to *the office* of President, however. He is only disqualified (by the Twenty-Second Amendment) from being *elected* to that office.

This is no mere semantic distinction. Article II of the Constitution carefully defines exactly who is "eligible to the Office of President": anyone who is a natural born citizen, at least 35 years old, and has been a U.S. resident for at least 14 years. For example, Secretary of State Madeleine Albright is ineligible for the office of President because she is a naturalized, rather than a natural born, citizen. Accordingly, the Twelfth Amendment renders her ineligible to the office of Vice President as well.

But Bill Clinton can serve as Vice President, because the Twenty-Second Amendment's prohibition on running for a third Presidential term is not a condition of the *office* of President. The Twenty-Second Amendment states: "No person shall be elected to the office of the President more than twice, and no person [who has served more than half a term] shall be elected to the office of the president more than once." The language is quite clear. It places no limits whatsoever on how many terms someone may *serve* as President—only how many times he can be *elected*.

In other words, the Twenty-Second Amendment does not set conditions on what the Twelfth Amendment calls eligibility to the office of President. Anyone who is born here and has lived here for fourteen years becomes eligible to be President on his or her thirty-fifth birthday—and is then so eligible forever.

Thus, if Clinton were to be elected Vice President, and ascend to the Presidency based on, for example, Mr. Gore's resignation, then nothing unconstitutional would have occurred. Clinton would have been *elected* to the Presidency only twice—

though he would *serve* as President thrice. Under the Twenty-Second Amendment, that is perfectly permissible.

The Spirit of the Twenty-second Amendment

Nonetheless, it could be argued that permitting Clinton to run for, and be elected to the office of, Vice President violates the spirit if not the letter of the Twenty-Second Amendment. The argument is a weak one, however. The Twenty-Second Amendment was adopted in part simply to formalize the tradition—unbroken until F.D.R.—that American Presidents should not seek a third term. It was also a reaction to the growth in the power of the President in the Twentieth Century. But in seeking the Vice-Presidency . . . Clinton would hardly be bidding for dictatorial powers.

Furthermore, Republicans trying to fend off the winning Gore-Clinton team lack standing to invoke the spirit of *any* constitutional provision, in preference to its plain language. George W. Bush proudly calls himself a "strict constructionist" who hews to the letter of the Constitution. And the exegesis of the Twenty-Second Amendment that I have provided here is exactly the sort of "textualism" that Bush judicial heroes [Supreme Court justices] Antonin Scalia and Clarence Thomas routinely applaud.

Of course, even if Gore were to offer him the number two spot, Clinton might turn it down. That would be a mistake for Clinton and for the country. He thrives on campaigns and we, as a people, thrive on him.

Congressional Term Limits Should Be Established

Edward H. Crane

Edward H. Crane argues in the following viewpoint that American citizens want a constitutional amendment that limits the term of office for members of Congress. Crane suggests that Congress should pass an amendment that will limit the term of state representatives to three terms in office. Such a limitation of tenure will ensure that those who serve in Congress will return to the private sector to live in the community for which they legislated, instead of remaining in political power indefinitely, removed from private citizenship. Crane argues that the American public wants a citizen legislature, one that governs as representatives of the people as the founding fathers intended. Crane further contends that a lack of term limits on Congress creates a "professionalization" that turns the legislative branch from a representative body to one of authority and hierarchy. Crane is the founder and president of the Cato Institute, a libertarian think-tank in Washington, D.C. His writings have been published in the Wall Street Journal, *the* Washington Post, *the* New York Times, *and* Forbes.

The term-limits movement is alive and well in the United States. Opponents of term limits, the most vociferous of whom live inside the Beltway [Washington, D.C.], had assumed the issue would go away following the Supreme Court's narrow five-to-four decision in *U.S. Term Limits v. Thornton* (1995) that said the states do not have the authority to limit the terms of their respective congressional delegations. As Justice Clarence Thomas pointed out in a brilliant dissent, the majority in *U.S. Term Limits* simply ignored the clear meaning

Edward H. Crane, "Term Limits and the Need for a Citizen Legislature," *CATO Handbook for Congress*, 1997. Copyright © 1997 by The CATO Institute. Republished with permission of CATO, conveyed through Copyright Clearance Center, Inc.

of the Tenth Amendment. There being no explicit denial of such power to the states in the Constitution, the right to do so "is reserved to the states respectively, or to the people."

Indeed, the people had spoken loudly and clearly on term limits in virtually all of the initiative states that provided them with an opportunity to do so. Twenty-two states representing nearly half of Congress had passed term limits on their delegations by 1994. The great majority of them had opted to limit their representatives to three terms, and all of them had limited their senators to two terms. Only 2 of the 22 states chose six terms for the House. That initiative process accurately reflected the views of the American people who support three-term limits for the House over six-term limits by a margin of five to one, according to a recent Luntz poll.

So intense is public support for a "citizen Congress" brought about through term limits—national polls have consistently put the number at 75 to 80 percent—that rather than give up after the Supreme Court's *U.S. Term Limits* decision, the movement instead intensified its efforts and adopted a new strategy. In November 1996 voters in nine states approved initiatives that instruct their congressional delegation to vote for term limits (defined as three terms in the House and two terms in the Senate) or face having placed next to their name on the ballot the words, "Disregarded voters' instructions on term limits."

The precedent for that ballot-language approach comes from the early 20th-century movement to end indirect election of senators by state legislatures. It worked, and in 1912 Congress complied with the will of the people by passing a constitutional amendment that called for the direct election of senators by the people. The parallels between the two movements are striking in that both were overwhelmingly popular throughout the nation, yet Congress had a clear conflict in terms of its own interests.

Given that precedent and the Supreme Court's reversal of the Arkansas Supreme Court's 1996 decision to remove a ballot-language initiative from its state ballot (the initiative, put back on the ballot by the Supreme Court, passed with 61 percent of the vote), it is very likely that ballot-language initiatives will be upheld as constitutional. And they will have an impact on candidates who do not support real term limits. . . .

Why Three Terms for the House?

It is important for Congress to address not just the issue of term limits but the nature of those limits. While those in Congress who purport to support term limits overwhelmingly favor six terms in the House, as noted above, the American people have stricter limits in mind. As Michael Kramer wrote in the January 23, 1995, issue of *Time*, "The dissonance between the people and their leaders on term limits is deafening." One possible compromise on this division, suggested by David Keating of the National Taxpayers Union, would be for Congress to vote out an amendment calling for a three-term limit for the House, but providing states with the option of increasing the House limit to six terms. U.S. Term Limits, the leading national term-limits organization, has indicated that such a compromise would be acceptable, thus potentially ending the long-standing split between the grassroots term-limits movement and term-limit supporters in Congress.

It is worth reviewing the reasons why the term-limits movement has been so adamant in supporting short, three-term limits for the House of Representatives, because the debate over three terms versus six terms is not mere quibbling over a technical issue. It is significant and substantive. It is a question of the people's term limits versus the politicians' disingenuous limits.

The political energy behind the term-limit movement is predicated on the need for a citizen legislature. Americans believe that career legislators and professional politicians have created a gaping chasm between themselves and their government. For democracy to work, it must be *representative* democracy—a government of, by, and for the people. That means a citizen legislature.

To achieve a citizen legislature it is imperative that our representatives in Congress—particularly in the House, which the Framers clearly intended to be the arm of government closest to the people—be not far removed from the private sector, which, after all, they are elected to represent. As Rhode Island's Roger Sherman wrote at the time of our nation's founding, "Representatives ought to return home and mix with the people. By remaining at the seat of government, they would acquire the habits of the place, which might differ from those of their constituents." In the era of year-round legislative sessions, the only way to achieve that objective is through term limits.

Three terms for the House is preferable to six terms for a variety of reasons. The most important one, however, deals with the question of who seeks to become a member of Congress in the first place. The fact is that America is best served by a Congress populated with members who are there out of a sense of civic duty, but who would rather live their lives in the private sector, holding productive jobs in civil society, outside the governmental world of political society. Such individuals might be willing to spend two, four, or even six years in Washington, but not if the legislative agenda is being set by others, who've gained their authority through seniority. Twelve-year "limits," which these days amount to a mini-career, do little to remove this major obstacle to a more diverse and representative group of Americans seeking office.

We already have hard evidence that short, three-term limits will enhance the democratic process: Proposition 140 in California, which was passed by the voters there in 1990 and limited the state Assembly to three two-year terms. The 1992 Assembly elections witnessed a sharp increase in the number of citizens seeking office, with a remarkable 27 freshmen elected in the 80-member lower house of the California legislature. In an article on that freshman class, the *Los Angeles Times* wrote, "Among the things making the group unusual is that most of them are true outsiders. For the first time in years, the freshman class does not include an abundance of former legislative aides who moved up the ladder to become members. . . . Among the 27 are a former U.S. Air Force fighter pilot, a former sheriff-coroner, a paralegal, a retired teacher, a video store owner, a businesswoman-homemaker, a children's advocate, an interior designer, a retired sheriff's lieutenant, and a number of businessmen, lawyers, and former city council members."

A 1996 scholarly study of the California legislature by Mark Petracca of the University of California at Irvine found that the strict term limits Californians passed in 1990 had had the following consequences:

- Turnover in both legislative chambers had increased markedly.

- The number of incumbents seeking reelection had dropped sharply.

- The percentage of elections in which incumbents won reelection had dropped significantly.

- The number of women in both houses had increased.

- The number of uncontested races had declined.

- The number of candidates seeking office in both chambers had increased.

- The winning margin of incumbents had declined.

All of those developments, while perhaps not attractive to those seeking to be career politicians, are consistent with the goals of the great majority of Americans who favor a return to a citizen legislature.

Similarly, a three-term limit for the U.S. House of Representatives will return control of the House—not just through voting, but through participation—to the people. We must make the possibility of serving in Congress a more attractive option for millions more Americans.

A second major reason for the need for a three-term limit is that it ensures that the majority of those serving in the House will not be far removed from their experiences in the private sector. They will bring to the policy issues of the day the common sense and practical experience of living in the real world that will lead to decisions that are truly in the public interest.

Many people reason that it has been the experienced legislators who have brought us the huge deficit and such undesirable episodes as the $300 billion savings-and-loan bailout [in the late 1980s]. The latter incident is a good example of why the common sense of Americans rooted in the private sector is needed in Congress. It's likely a Congress picked by lottery would have refused to expand federal deposit insurance as part of the necessary move to deregulate the thrift industry. "Inexperienced" legislators would have said, in effect, yes, do deregulate, but for goodness sake don't ask the American taxpayer to pay for any bad investments the thrift institutions make—that's a license to speculate. But our experienced legislators apparently thought they could repeal the laws of economics, raising the level of federal deposit insurance and extending it to the deposit rather than the depositor, thus allowing the wealthiest people in the nation to spread their deposits around with utter indifference to the financial soundness of the institutions in which they invested. We are still paying the price for such legislative hubris.

A third reason for the shorter limits is related to the second. And that is that the longer one is in Congress, the more one is exposed to and influenced by the "culture of ruling" that permeates life inside the Beltway. Groups like the Na-

Limiting Terms in the Senate and Congress

In 2005, nine hundred registered voters nationwide were asked: "Do you favor or oppose limiting the number of terms members of the U.S. Senate and House of Representatives, including your own senators and representatives, can serve?"

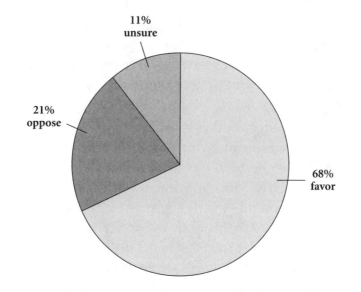

11%
unsure

21%
oppose

68%
favor

TAKEN FROM: Fox News/Opinion Dyamics Poll, June 14–15, 2005.
www.pollingreport.com.

tional Taxpayers Union have documented the fact that the longer people serve in Congress, the bigger spenders and regulators they become. That is just as true of conservatives as it is of liberals. It is also understandable. Members of Congress are surrounded at work and socially by people whose jobs are to spend other people's money and regulate their lives. It is the unusual individual—although such people do exist—who is not subtly but surely affected by that culture.

A fourth reason to support three terms over six terms is that the shorter limits are an antidote to the growing "professionalization" of the legislative process. As Mark Petracca has written, "Whereas representative government aspires to maintain a proximity of sympathy and interests between representative and represented, professionalism creates authority, autonomy, and hierarchy, distancing the expert from the client. Though this distance may be necessary and functional for lawyers, nurses, physicians, accountants, and social scientists, the qualities and characteristics associated with being a 'professional' legislator run counter to the supposed goals of a representative democracy. Professionalism encourages an independence of ambition, judgment, and behavior that is squarely at odds with the inherently dependent nature of representative government."

Competitiveness and Diversity

Finally, the shorter limits for the House are guaranteed to enhance the competitiveness of elections and, as noted above, increase the number and diversity of Americans choosing to run for Congress. As Paul Jacob of U.S. Term Limits has pointed out, the most competitive races (and the ones that bring out the largest number of primary candidates) are for open seats. At least a third of all House seats will be open each election under three-term limits, and it is probable that as many as half will not feature an incumbent seeking reelection. We also know from past experience that women and minorities have greater electoral success in races for open seats.

The incentives for a citizen legislature are significantly stronger under the shorter limits. Six-term limits are long enough to induce incumbents to stick around for the entire 12 years. Three-term limits are short enough to prompt incumbents to return to the private sector before spending six years in the House. Under a three-term limit we will witness a return to the 19th-century norm of half the House being freshmen—a true citizen legislature.

In addition, the next most competitive races are incumbents' first attempts at reelection and the races just before retirement. Thus, under a three-term limit virtually all races for the House of Representatives will be more competitive than is the case today or would be the case under six-term limits.

In order for the concept of a citizen legislature to have meaning, it is imperative that those serving in the legislature literally view their time in office as a leave of absence from their real jobs or careers. That is the key to a successful citizen legislature. The incentives facing a member of Congress should never include concern about what other legislators might do in retaliation, or what special interests might do to the member's political career.

In the introductory essay in *The Politics and Law of Term Limits,* coauthors Ed Crane and Roger Pilon wrote, "Stepping back from these policy arguments, however, one sees a deeper issue in the term-limits debate, an issue that takes us to our very foundations as a nation. No one can doubt that America was dedicated to the proposition that each of us is and ought to be free—free to plan, and live his own life, as a private individual, under a government instituted to secure that freedom. Thus, implicit in our founding vision is the idea that most human affairs take place in what today we call the private sector. That sector—and this is the crucial point—is primary: government comes from it, not the other way around. When we send men and women to Congress to 'represent' us, therefore, we want them to understand that they represent us, the overwhelming number of Americans who live our daily lives in that private sector. Moreover, we want them to remember that it is to that private world that they must return, to live under the laws they have made as our representatives. That, in essence, is the message implicit in the growing call for term limits. It is not simply or even primarily a message about 'good government.' Rather, it is a message about the very place of government in the larger scheme of things. Government is meant to be our servant, to assist us by securing our liberty as we live our essentially private lives. It is not meant to be our master in some grand public adventure."

The term-limits movement is not motivated by disdain for the institution of Congress. It is motivated by a sincere desire on the part of the American people to regain control of the most representative part of the federal government. The people want term limits and for good reasons. Resistance to this movement on the part of elected federal legislators only underscores the image of an Imperial Congress.

Consistency and Experience Should Override New York City's Term Limits Law

Michael Bloomberg

In the following viewpoint, New York City mayor Michael Bloomberg discusses why he thinks he should be allowed to run for a third term in office, even though the law in New York City limits the mayor's time in office to two four-year terms. Bloomberg argues that in the difficult financial times facing the United States and the city of New York, his background in finance and business will help pull the city out of financial hardship. He further contends that by continuing as mayor of New York, he will be better suited than anyone else to handle the challenges the city faces, since he has done the job for eight years and knows firsthand the workings of the city council. Bloomberg further states that much work needs to be done to improve the city's school system, infrastructure, housing, and public health services, and he feels that his job as mayor of New York City is not yet done.

Bloomberg was elected to his third term as mayor of New York City in 2009.

As everyone knows who's worked side by side with me for the past seven years, I love this city [New York City]—as a place to raise my family, to build my business from scratch, to give back—and I've loved every day that I have served as mayor. There is no greater honor than being able to make a difference in people's lives and for me that's what public service really is all about.

Today, our nation and our City, as you know, face unprecedented challenges. As a businessman with expertise on Wall

Michael Bloomberg, "Mayor Bloomberg Addresses New Yorkers About Term Limits," New York City Government, October 2, 2008. Copyright © 2008 The City of New York. Reproduced by permission.

New York City mayor Michael Bloomberg campaigns in Brooklyn for a third term in March 2009. He was re-elected in November 2009. AP Images.

Street and finance, and as a mayor who has balanced budgets and delivered services, I can tell you that the enormity of the challenges ahead should not be underestimated.

On the national stage, there will be no easy fixes. We can debate forever how our nation got here, but make no mistake about it, the $700 billion bailout is not a magic bullet; it's a badly needed, short-term, stop-gap measure but it will by no means make all our problems disappear.

This is not a time for fantasy; that's what helped get our nation into the mess we now confront. The consequences for New York City are very real. Some of our largest employers and most established companies are in turmoil—and others don't even exist anymore. The good news is we have planned for a slow down in New York, but we may well be on the verge of a meltdown, and it's up to us to rise to the occasion.

In recent weeks and months, as you know, I've listened to many different New Yorkers with lots of different opinions on the issue of term limits. But as our economic situation has become increasingly unstable, the question for me has become far less about the theoretical and much more about the practical.

And so to put it in very practical terms: handling this financial crisis while strengthening essential services—such as education and public safety—is a challenge I want to take on for the people of New York. And so, should the City Council vote to amend term limits, I plan to ask New Yorkers to look at my record of independent leadership—and then to decide if I have earned another term. As always, it will be up to the people to decide, not me.

In thinking about the challenges ahead, beyond the direct challenge of managing the financial crisis, I have asked myself: do we have more work to do in transforming the schools, greening the environment, building vital infrastructure and record amounts of affordable housing, improving public health, investing in long-term economic growth? And the list goes on. And the answer is: yes, we do have more to do, a lot more.

Of course, there will always be more to do—I understand that. But there are times when you know a job is done and times when you feel like you're in the thick of major changes that still require hard work and careful management and tough accountability. I care deeply about sustaining the progress we've made—and finishing the job voters elected me to do.

Now, I also understand that people voted for a two-term limit, and altering their verdict is not something that I think should be done lightly. But as newspaper editorialists and others have pointed out, the current law denies voters the right to choose who to vote for—at a time when our economy is in turmoil and the Council is a democratically elected representative body.

The Charter allows the Council to change the law—and it doesn't favor one method of adoption over another. Speaker [Christine C.] Quinn has always done a great job of soliciting public input and making decisions that may not be easy or popular, but that she believes to be right. And I have directed my staff to work with her staff to produce a new term limits bill. If the Council passes it, I will sign it—and I would plan to run for re-election.

Given the events of recent weeks and given the enormous challenges we face, I don't want to walk away from a city I feel I can help lead through these tough times. My whole life has prepared me for the challenges ahead and I want to give the voters a chance to decide if they want me at the helm. If voters don't like what they've seen, they will vote for someone else and that's as it should be. But whatever the Council does, I'll remain focused on my job and serving New Yorkers and the city I love.

The New York City Council Violated the Will of the People by Overturning the City's Term Limits Law

Michael D. Roberts

In the following viewpoint, Michael D. Roberts discusses the overturning of New York City's two-term law, which will allow incumbent mayor Michael Bloomberg (and city council members) to run for an additional term. Roberts contends that the New York City Council disregarded the will of New Yorkers—who voted twice in the 1990s to preserve term limits for the city's mayoral seat—in voting by a 29 to 22 margin in favor of allowing Bloomberg to run for a third term in the 2009 election. Roberts argues that by approving Bloomberg's request to seek a third term, city council members are acting in self-preservation of their own lucrative jobs, rather than in the best interest of city residents. Roberts alludes to the Twenty-second Amendment to the U.S. Constitution, which limits the president of the United States to two terms in office, stating that term limits—whether in federal or local government—are not new. He asserts that the city council's actions have made New York's mayoral seat resemble a monarchy, as the city council disregarded the people's decision to keep term limits in place.

Roberts is editor of New York Carib News.

By a vote of 29 to 22 the New York City Council rubber-stamped billionaire Mayor Mike Bloomberg's legal end-run around term limits and gave him—and themselves—a term extension of four more years. In the end, principle and the will of the people was trumped as term-limited members

Michael D. Roberts, "New York City's Term Limits—Hail King Mike!" *New York Carib News*, October 29, 2008. Reproduced by permission.

who joined with the mayor and his supporters voted to preserve their $112,500 a year jobs, which the council increased from $90,000 in late 2006. Apparently, in these challenging economic times the mayor's political gambit and four more years of a six-figure income and perks were just too tempting to pass up.

But the vote demonstrates just how divisive and contentious this issue is and Mayor Bloomberg may just have bought a new torrid term in office. [City Council] Speaker Christine Quinn and others who sided with the Mayor are now perceived as "in the mayor's pocket" and by this vote the City Council has been severely weakened since it failed its first major political test of wills. The Council ignored and rendered irrelevant the "will of the voters" and bowed to mayoral bullying in a show of total political cowardice and financial self-preservation.

Term limits and tinkering with it is nothing new. And it has not been confined only to local politics. In fact, the 22nd Amendment to the United States Constitution was passed in 1951 to make sure that no U.S. president—after Franklin D. Roosevelt—ever served more than eight years in office. Now, 57 years later, New York City's Mayor Mike Bloomberg is seeking a third term in office after New Yorkers voted twice to keep term limits in place.

The issue has opened heated public debate over the fact that a majority of the members of the City Council—where 38 of its 51 members are term-limited—sided with the mayor to do an end run around the term limits law by passing its own law that extends the mayor's term—and the 38 term-limited members—for another four years, thus giving them three terms in office. The reality is that the City Council has legally extended term limits without a public referendum and the Mayor banked on the fact that the Council's members would buck public anger and outrage and preserve their well-paying part-time jobs.

As the supporters of the mayor and himself spin it, he's the best person to guide New York City through the present financial crisis because of his fiscal experience. This suggests that nobody in the city's 8.5 million inhabitants can do better or possess these skills. That is not only insulting but an arrogant predisposition to setting up what literally amounts to an elected monarchy. Hail King Mike I!

Under Mayor Mike Bloomberg's "leadership," the city has lost tens of thousands of jobs in recent months as the financial crisis has gripped Wall Street. Under his "leadership," the city is facing tough times, times that might call for a new mayor. But the mayor's supporters say that he knows best. Oh, and what about those pesky voters who approved term limits twice in the past—twice have approved two-term limits?

Well, the *Daily News, New York Times* and the *New York Post* all say that the City Council will just have to override the voters because, after all, politicians know best. Term limits were originally proposed as an antidote to the power of incumbency in New York City politics. In 1993 there was a referendum on the ballot to create term limits in New York City. New Yorkers voted for term limits by an overwhelming majority.

In 1996, the City Council put a referendum on the ballot that would extend term limits to three terms instead of two. This second referendum was defeated by the voters, so the two-term limit remained. In 2001, term limits took effect. The mayor, comptroller, and public advocate, four of five borough presidents, and 38 of 51 council members were term-limited out of office. Now, two terms later, in 2009, the people who were first elected in 2001 are seeing term limits of their own.

The arguments for extending term limits, particularly in the context of Mayor Bloomberg's position, is that it will remove the most experienced people from City government, that it will strengthen the role of lobbyists and government staffers, that it will weaken the legislative branch of government, create politicians who are more concerned about their next job than serving others and if voters want to remove an unpopular political leader they can do so at the next election.

On the other hand, supporters of term limits argue that it brings fresh views and opinions to government, will make representatives more responsive to people, help eliminate abuses that come with unlimited power and, ultimately, will help overcome the insurmountable advantages of incumbency and make elections much more competitive.

All that may be very well true but there are two problems with this new round of term limit ups and downs. The first is that the mayor's timing is very, very bad indeed, because this last-minute tactic to stay in office smacks of a naked power grab and an attitude that reeks of arrogance and disregard for the city's voters. Had he floated this idea at the start of his second term—and not at the end—then he could make a far better case to the people.

Second, there is the little annoyance that New Yorkers already voted in favor of term limits—twice. Opponents say that the mayor, in collusion with the City Council, is undermining the decision and will of the people. By cutting the public out of the process, such a move is inherently unfair and undemocratic. Moreover, this legislative action is not the only course that the Mayor and City Council can take to bring democracy to this issue.

The mayor sees a special election as an unnecessary irritant to his ambitions. There is still time to put this matter to the people of New York City for a vote, and that will ensure that New Yorkers have the opportunity to voice their opinions on this matter at the polls. There is indeed still plenty of time to establish a Charter Revision Commission and to put this question on the ballot at a special election referendum as early as this winter [2008–2009]. This can all be completed before the elections next fall [November 2009].

But here is also an issue of public perception as to the independence and effectiveness of the City Council in relation to the mayor. Is the City Council simply a reliable tool to be used by the mayor whenever he wants to circumvent the will of the people? Is it a rubber stamp for his ambition, policies and thus a toothless, spineless body of mighty talkers only bent on preserving their lucrative, well-paid part-time jobs?

Term limits may be good or bad and there are valid arguments on both sides of the issue. However, in this case people are angry about the way that the mayor [flouted] the issue and the kind of political arm-twisting that went into this vote. New Yorkers are divided over the merits or demerits of term limits, that is why the democratic and principled approach should be a public referendum—not a coronation of a new king who simply woke up one morning and decided that regardless of what New Yorkers felt he could override it and stay in office as long as he wanted.

By acting legislatively on the issue of extending term limits as opposed to going back to the voters, the power of the City Council will be greatly diminished. Surrendering to the will or dictates of the mayor will give the general public the idea that it is a cowardly, easily manipulated and divided Council that does not and cannot be relied upon to protect and defend the interests of "we the people."

Reversing two referenda approved by millions of voters in the 1990s, the Council and those who voted with Mayor Bloomberg acted in collusion with his unbridled political ambition and dictatorial attitude ultimately subverting and usurping the will of its own constituencies.

Appendix

Appendix

The Amendments to the U.S. Constitution

Amendment I: Freedom of Religion, Speech, Press, Petition, and
                  Assembly (ratified 1791)
Amendment II: Right to Bear Arms (ratified 1791)
Amendment III: Quartering of Soldiers (ratified 1791)
Amendment IV: Freedom from Unfair Search and Seizures
                  (ratified 1791)
Amendment V: Right to Due Process (ratified 1791)
Amendment VI: Rights of the Accused (ratified 1791)
Amendment VII: Right to Trial by Jury (ratified 1791)
Amendment VIII: Freedom from Cruel and Unusual Punishment
                  (ratified 1791)
Amendment IX: Construction of the Constitution (ratified 1791)
Amendment X: Powers of the States and People (ratified 1791)
Amendment XI: Judicial Limits (ratified 1795)
Amendment XII: Presidential Election Process (ratified 1804)
Amendment XIII: Abolishing Slavery (ratified 1865)
Amendment XIV: Equal Protection, Due Process, Citizenship for All
                  (ratified 1868)

The Amendments to the U.S. Constitution

Amendment XV: Race and the Right to Vote (ratified 1870)

Amendment XVI: Allowing Federal Income Tax (ratified 1913)

Amendment XVII: Establishing Election to the U.S. Senate (ratified 1913)

Amendment XVIII: Prohibition (ratified 1919)

Amendment XIX: Granting Women the Right to Vote (ratified 1920)

Amendment XX: Establishing Term Commencement for Congress and the President (ratified 1933)

Amendment XXI: Repeal of Prohibition (ratified 1933)

Amendment XXII: Establishing Term Limits for U.S. President (ratified 1951)

Amendment XXIII: Allowing Washington, D.C., Representation in the Electoral College (ratified 1961)

Amendment XXIV: Prohibition of the Poll Tax (ratified 1964)

Amendment XXV: Presidential Disability and Succession (ratified 1967)

Amendment XXVI: Lowering the Voting Age (ratified 1971)

Amendment XXVII: Limiting Congressional Pay Increases (ratified 1992)

For Further Research

Books

Sunil Ahuja and Robert E. Dewhirst, eds., *Congress Responds to the Twentieth Century.* Columbus: Ohio State University Press, 2003.

Jeremy D. Bailey, *Thomas Jefferson and Executive Power.* New York: Cambridge University Press, 2007.

James K. Coyne and John H. Fund, *Cleaning House: America's Campaign for Term Limits.* Washington, DC: National Book Network, 1992.

David A. Crockett, *The Opposition Presidency: Leadership and the Constraints of History.* College Station: Texas A&M University Press, 2002.

Barbara Silberdick Feinberg, *Term Limits for Congress?* New York: Twenty-First Century Books, 1996.

James R. Hedtke, *The Effects of the Twenty-second Amendment on Presidential Power: A Critical Examination of the Lame Duck Syndrome.* PhD diss., Philadelphia: Temple University, 1998.

Michael H. Klein, *The Twenty-second Amendment: Term Limitation in the Executive Branch.* Washington, DC: Americans to Limit Congressional Terms, 1989.

David E. Kyvig, ed., *Unintended Consequences of Constitutional Amendment.* Athens: University of Georgia Press, 2000.

Ronald W. Reagan et al., *Restoring the Presidency: Reconsidering the Twenty-second Amendment.* Washington, DC: National Legal Center for the Public Interest, 1990.

Gary L. Rose, *The American Presidency Under Siege.* Albany: State University of New York Press, 1997.

Marjorie Sarbaugh-Thompson et al., *The Political and Institutional Effects of Term Limits*. New York: Palgrave Macmillan, 2004.

Charles W. Stein, *The Third-Term Tradition: Its Rise and Collapse in American Politics*. New York: Columbia University Press, 1972.

James L. Sundquist, *Constitutional Reform and Effective Government*. Washington, DC: Brookings Institution, 1992.

John R. Vile, *A Companion to the United States Constitution and Its Amendments*. Westport, CT: Praeger, 2006.

Periodicals

James MacGregor Burns and Susan Dunn, "No More Second-Term Blues," *New York Times*, January 5, 2006.

David A. Crockett and Kevin Bruyneel, "Should the 22nd Amendment Be Repealed?" *New York Times Upfront*, April 24, 2006.

Bruce G. Peabody, "George Washington, Presidential Term Limits, and the Problem of Reluctant Political Leadership," *Presidential Studies Quarterly*, vol. 31, no. 3, September 2001.

Bruce G. Peabody and Scott E. Gant, "The Twice and Future President: Constitutional Interstices and the Twenty-second Amendment," *Minnesota Law Review*, February 1999.

Cal Thomas, "How to End the Lame-Duck Rut," *USA Today*, October 12, 2005.

Jonathan Zimmerman, "Abolish Presidential Term Limits," *Christian Science Monitor*, December 27, 2006.

Internet Sources

Eric Green, "Term Limits Help Prevent Dictatorships: Attempts to Repeal U.S. Two-Term Law Not Succeeding," *America.gov*, August 27, 2007. www.america.gov.

WorldnetDaily.com, "Should Presidents Be Allowed to Serve More than Two Terms? Bills Introduced in Congress to Repeal 8-year Restriction of 22nd Amendment," October 8, 2006. www.worldnetdaily.com.

Web Sites

Cato Institute, www.cato.org. The Cato Institute provides the transcript of a 2001 policy forum titled "Term Limits and American Government," which discusses Amendment XXII and its impact on the presidencies of Ronald Reagan and Bill Clinton.

Justice Learning, www.justicelearning.org. Justice Learning provides the wording of Amendment XXII and an interpretation of the amendment in terms that young readers can understand. It also provides a timeline of the amendment's ratification and events leading up to its passage.

National Constitution Center, www.constitutioncenter.org. The National Constitution Center presents *Centuries of Citizenship: A Constitutional Timeline,* an online experience that recounts key events that helped shape the U.S. Constitution. Online visitors can browse a collection of stories and headlines to learn how events in American history have had an effect on the Constitution.

Index

H

Hamilton, Alexander, 15, 32, 101–102, 106, 109–113
Harrison, William Henry, 34
Hayes, Rutherford B., 47, 108
Henry, Laurin, 118
Hill, Lister, 87
Howell, William G., 115–126

I

Ickes, Harold, 75–76
International agreements, 123–125
International Criminal Court (ICC), 124–125

J

Jackson, Andrew, 33, 47, 83, 108
Jacob, Paul, *75*, 139
Jefferson, Thomas
    precedent set by, 33, 83
    on term limits, 14, 45–46, 108–110
Johnson, Lyndon B., 19

K

Kallenbach, Joseph E., 29–41
Keating, David, 134
Keating, Kenneth, 87
Koenig, Louis, 80
Koh, Harold Hongju, 117
Kramer, Michael, 134

L

Lame duck presidency, 18, 97, 105–126
Legislative branch, 38–39, 80, 138–139
Legislative election, of president, 32–33

Lemelin, Bernard, 72–81
Lincoln, Abraham, 83
Lucas, Scott W., 86, 87
Lyle, John, 87

M

Madison, James, 108
Madison, Marbury v., 116
Mansfield, Mike, 94–99
Marbury v. Madison, 116
Martin, Joseph, 16, 72–73, 80
Mason, George, 32
Mayer, Kenneth R., 115–126
McCoy, Donald, 79
McKinley, William, 48
Michener, Earl, 16, 84
Monroe, James, 108
Morse, Wayne, 89

N

National Committee Against Limiting the Presidency, 72–81
National emergencies, 71, 112–113
National monuments, 122–123
New Deal, 77
New York City
    term limits law should be overridden, 142–145
    term limits should not be overturned, 146–150
New York Times, 69–71
Norris, George W., 61
Norton, Gale, 123

O

O'Daniel, W. Lee, 88

28.60   10/14/10